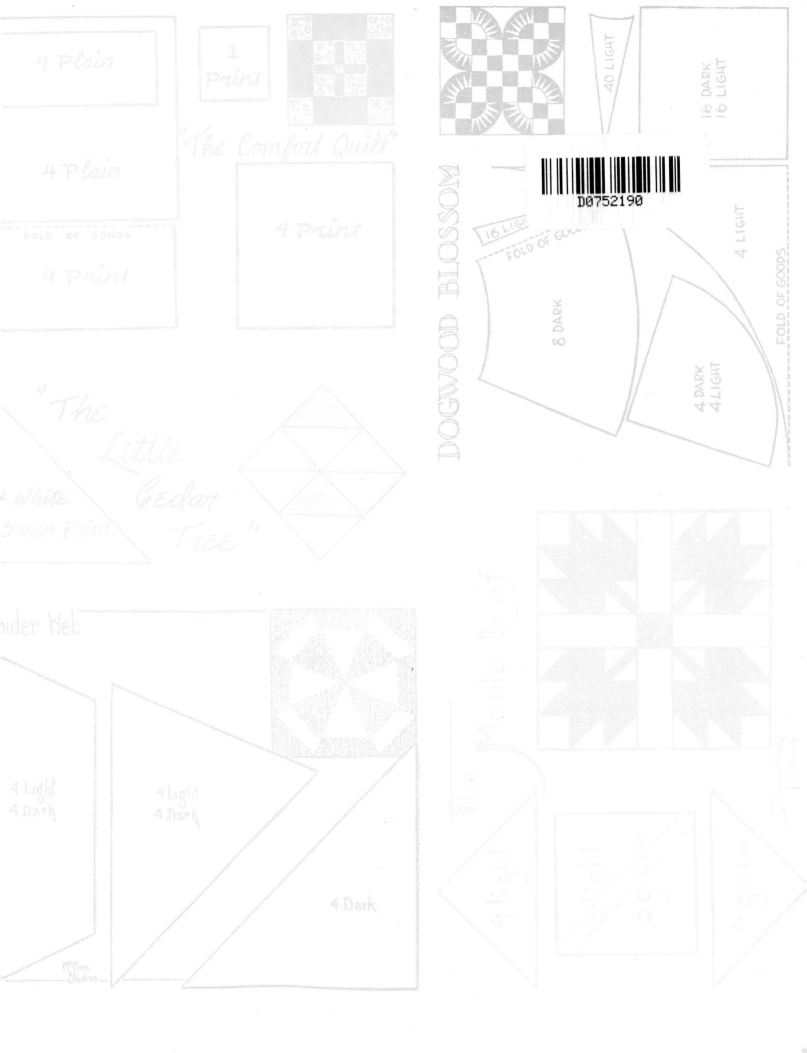

PATTERNS OF HISTORY

The Challenge Winners

23 Quilt Designs Inspired by Our Past

BY KATHY DELANEY

PATTERNS OF HISTORY
The Challenge Winners
23 Quilt Designs Inspired by Our Past

By KATHY DELANEY

Acknowledgments

PATTERNS OF HISTORY
The Challenge Winners
23 Quilt Designs Inspired by Our Past

By Kathy Delaney
Edited By Evie Rapport

Book design and production by Jo Ann Groves
Photography by Bill Krzyzanowski and Kathy Delaney
Templates by Eric Sears, Gary Embrey Design

Published by Kansas City Star Books
1729 Grand Blvd., Kansas City, Missouri 64108
Copyright © 2005 by The Kansas City Star. Co.

First Edition, first printing
ISBN-10: 1-933466-06-5
ISBN-13: 978-1-933466-06-4
Printed in the United States of America
by Walsworth Publishing Co.
To order copies, call StarInfo, (816) 234-4696
and say "Books."

KANSAS CITY STAR BOOKS

What an interesting project this has been! I wish to thank Doug Weaver for the opportunity to work with these wonderful quilts. When he asked if I would like to write this book, I jumped in with both feet! At times I was overwhelmed, but each new quilt was reason to get excited all over again.

I wish to thank Bill Krzyzanowski for his photography skills, which reveal the inner life of a quilt. Evie Rapport, and her watchful eye, found my mistakes, cheered me on and generally kept me going. Thanks, Evie! Jo Ann Groves did the original design work on the *Patterns of History* contest booklet. Her expertise created this very usable book. Jo Ann is the greatest!

Thank you, Barbara Brackman for writing the foreword to this work. What an honor. And thank you, Edie McGinnis, Deb Rowden and Terry Thompson for taking time from your busy quilting and writing schedules to help choose the winning quilts.

Mostly I want to thank all the quilters who entered this contest. It was not easy to choose just 23 quilts from all the entries. The quilters really met the challenge and created some wonderful quilts. Even though we had to limit the book to the three winners and 20 honorable-mention quilts, each quilt submitted would make a great addition. It is just too bad books are not able to have an unlimited number of pages!

I wish to thank all the quilters who are inspired by these quilts. It is for you we work to share the art of quiltmaking. May all your quilts be winning quilts!

Kathy Delaney

Table of Contents

PATTERNS OF HISTORY

Foreword

Quilt contests were big news in the 1930s and 1940s. Newspapers, department stores and expositions transformed the traditional competitions familiar at county fairs into national events. In the days when flagpole sitters and marathon dance contests fascinated newspaper readers, quilt shows received similar attention. "Liberty Quilt Show Acclaimed Greatest Ever Held in United States," shouted the headline in a Kentucky newspaper.

Barbara

Organizers offered ribbons, certificates, quilting cottons and trophy cups for the oldest, the most beautiful or the best-made quilt, but during the Depression's tough times, cash prizes were strong incentive. Quilters familiar with the usual $1 premium at the local fair were awed by the prizes listed in the national contests. The annual Eastern States Exposition at Storrowton, Mass., offered numerous $50 prizes for both antique and modern quilts, attracting entrants from around the country. Quilters hoped to win the $100 first prize in a 1939 event sponsored by the National Federation of Press Women. The most impressive prize was the promised $1,200 at the 1933 Chicago World's Fair, an award that drew 25,000 entrants.

In the spirit of those contests from the quilt fad of the early 20th century, United Notion's Moda Fabrics and *The Kansas City Star* decided to sponsor a competition in 2004, "Patterns of History 1930-1950: Pick a Pack—Pick a Pattern." We added a modern twist, making it a quilt challenge as well as a contest.

In a quilt challenge, restrictions concerning theme, fabric or color add a structure to a competition. We included both fabric and pattern guidelines, requiring that entrants use a good proportion of fabric from the reproduction collection Patterns of History co-produced by Moda and *The Star*.

We picked five pieced patterns from *The Star's* quilt column during the quilt mania of the 1930s and '40s and asked that the quilters begin with one of those. The five included beginner-level designs such as the Comfort Quilt and the Little Cedar Tree, based on simple squares, rectangles and triangles. We also chose more complex designs, such as the Spider Web, which demands careful piecing to match eight central points, and the Dogwood Blossom with its arc pieced of tiny points.

We also wanted to represent the three designers who edited *The Star's* quilt column during that golden age of newspaper patterns. Ruby Short McKim, Edna Marie Dunn and Eveline Foland are each represented by a block typical of her style.

Challenges always offer surprising results because they force creative people to work within new structures. Enjoy the quilts in this book. They give us the opportunity to see the many ways that 23 clever quilters worked within the same guidelines, allowing us to share their individual views of fabric and pattern.

Barbara Brackman

Introduction

There is nothing better than a challenge. It tests us, makes us work all the harder to do well and often surprises us by the outcome. A quilt challenge is the best! It stretches us, makes us creative and lets us use techniques we've been wanting to try but that caused us hesitation or made us reluctant to start yet another large project.

When quilt historian and author Barbara Brackman; Doug Weaver, publisher of Kansas City Star Books at *The Kansas City Star*, long a source for patterns to quilters all over the Midwest; and Moda Fabrics, one of the quilting world's favorite makers of quilting cottons, got together and created the challenge "Patterns of History 1930-1950: Pick a Pack—Pick a Pattern," quilters everywhere were invited to stretch, create and win.

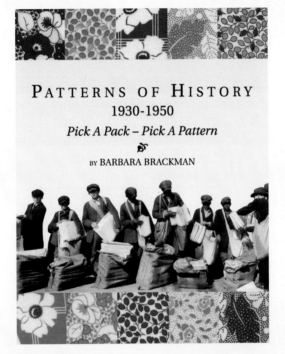

Photographs of the entry quilts were studied by the judges: Doug Weaver of *The Kansas City Star*, Kathy Delaney, Edie McGinnis, Deb Rowden and Terry Thompson – Star Quilt book authors all – and the winning quilts were chosen.

I love mysteries and I love puzzles, almost as much as I love a challenge! When I was asked to write the patterns for the winning quilts, I jumped at the challenge of figuring out how the entrants made their quilts.

In this book you will find photographs of the winning quilts as well as directions so that you may create your own version. Now, the directions may not reflect the exact way the quilter made the original. By measuring the finished quilts and choosing techniques I would use, I have written instructions that will allow you to duplicate the quilts fairly closely. As you work, you may even find that techniques with which you are familiar can be substituted. However you do it, I hope you have fun creating these winning quilts.

Following the original patterns, you will find the three winning quilts arranged in order, followed by the Honorable Mention winners. These are arranged alphabetically by the quilter's last name, because the last of these quilts is no "less" than the first.

Every effort has been made on the patterns so that you can re-create the quilts as closely as possible, using techniques that are the easiest. It is assumed that quilters using this book have some experience, and some basic knowledge is implied. The fabric requirements for the projects will include enough fabric to accommodate mistakes in cutting so you don't have to worry about purchasing extra "just in case." And the fabrics will include color references to the prize-winning quilt so you can see exactly which fabric is which.

Unless otherwise noted, all strips are to be cut across the grain of the fabric, selvage to selvage. All cutting instructions are based on the assumption that there is 40" of usable fabric after the selvages have been removed. You may find the fabric you use is wider. Seam allowances are to be sewn 1/4".

We hope you have as much fun with this challenge as we did.

The Judges

Kathy Delaney is a designer, author and national quilting teacher. In fact, her favorite part of her passion for quilts is teaching, and her books reflect this.

Kathy

A seamstress since the age of 10, Kathy has always had a love of fabric, color and texture. Her degree in art education formed the groundwork for her becoming a quiltmaker and designer.

While she does not have a family connection with quilts, Kathy has taken to the art with a consistent passion. On any given day, she can be found thinking about her next quilt, shopping for fabric for a new quilt, stitching on one of many current quilts, writing about quilt-making techniques, sketching plans for a new appliqué design, attending a guild meeting, lecturing about or teaching quilt making. In fact, her husband does not believe she does anything but make quilts. He might be right!

This is Kathy's fifth book for Kansas City Star Books.

Edie McGinnis is an author and editor with a unique perspective: She is a member of *The Kansas City Star* staff. Since she went to work there in April 1987, she has been an advocate for the revival of *The Star's* tradition of publishing quilt blocks.

Edie

She is now part of the Star Books staff and has written seven quilt books. She is working on her eighth and has ideas for many more. She writes a column for *The Star's* Quilt web site, PickleDish.com. *The Star* has also published single patterns of two quilts Edie has designed.

Edie lectures on *The Kansas City Star* quilt patterns, their history and the designers who worked at the newspaper when the patterns were published. She has been quilting since the mid-1970s and is a member of the American Quilting Society and the Quilters Guild of Greater Kansas City.

Debra Gehlbach Rowden enjoys combining her passion for words and fabric at every opportunity. She is the author of two Kansas City Star quilt books: *Quilters' Stories: Collecting History in the Heart of America* and, with Frances Kite, *Quilting a Poem: Original Designs Inspired by America's Most Beloved Poets*. She is also the author of *Susan McCord: The Unforgettable Artistry of an Indiana Quilter* with Barbara Brackman and Shauna Christensen. She made her first quilt in 1973 and has a degree in mass communications/clothing and textiles from Kansas State University.

Debra

Deb meets weekly with a small quilt group, the Women Who Run With Scissors, and is a member of the Kaw Valley Quilters' Guild. She lives in her hometown of Lawrence, Kan., which she happily considers a hotbed of creativity.

Terry Thompson, born into the fifth generation of a Kansas pioneer family, has been on the forefront of our current quilt revival. Her stitching passion began when she sewed calico dresses for her daughter. With the leftover scraps, she made a quilt.

Terry

In 1973 Terry opened the Quilting Bee, an anomaly at the time: a store devoted totally to quilting. The shop was located on the historic Country Club Plaza of Kansas City, Mo., until 1984.

Besides designing appliqué patterns, Terry has written six books, each a collection of family stories in different eras with quilts designed to complement the stories. She also designs a line of reproduction fabric for Moda with Barbara Brackman.

Doug Weaver is the publisher of *The Kansas City Star* quilt-book series and oversees the overall direction of *The Star's* quilt efforts. Doug joined *The Star* in 1987 and has had a several roles,

Doug

including Business editor, editor for Readership and New Initiatives and director of Strategic Business Development. He now directs the newspaper's book-publishing and retail-merchandising efforts of which Star Quilts is a part.

The Winners

Patricia S. Beck won FIRST PLACE for her quilt "Through the Window"

Patricia Heath won SECOND PLACE for her quilt "My Grandmothers Kitchen"

Peggy Thackston won THIRD PLACE for her quilt "Blue Dogwood Trail"

HONORABLE MENTIONS were awarded to:

Kathryn Botsford for her quilt "Dogwood Reflections"

Annie Brasseal for her quilt "Dogwood Festival"

Linda Carlson for her quilt "A Garden Wall"

Tara Didier and Melissa Ulmen for their quilt "Aunt Niece's Cedar Tree"

Rita J. Feely for her quilt "Dream Weaver"

Judy Hitchcock for her quilt "XO"

Maxine Kline for her quilt "Springtime in the Cedars"

Linda Birch Mooney for her quilt "Honoring those Kansas City Designing Women"

Jane Morse for her quilt "Murphy's Law"

Terry Pottmeyer for her quilt "Tidings of Comfort"

Angie G. Purvis for her quilt "Hope…"

Jennifer S. Riggs for her quilt "Maple Leaf Swirl"

Marilyn Robertson for her quilt "'40s Comfort"

Barbara A. Roidt for her quilt "Kansas City Star"

Nancy Romine for her quilt "Sunshine on Ruby's Tulips"

Wendy Sticken for her quilt "Spring in Bloom"

Marlys Tillman for her quilt "Red Paintbrush"

Annie Unrein for her quilt "Dogwood Do Si Do"

Kimberly Weingart for her quilt "Shaker Tree"

Dorothy Ziegler for her quilt "Dogwood Trail"

The Patterns

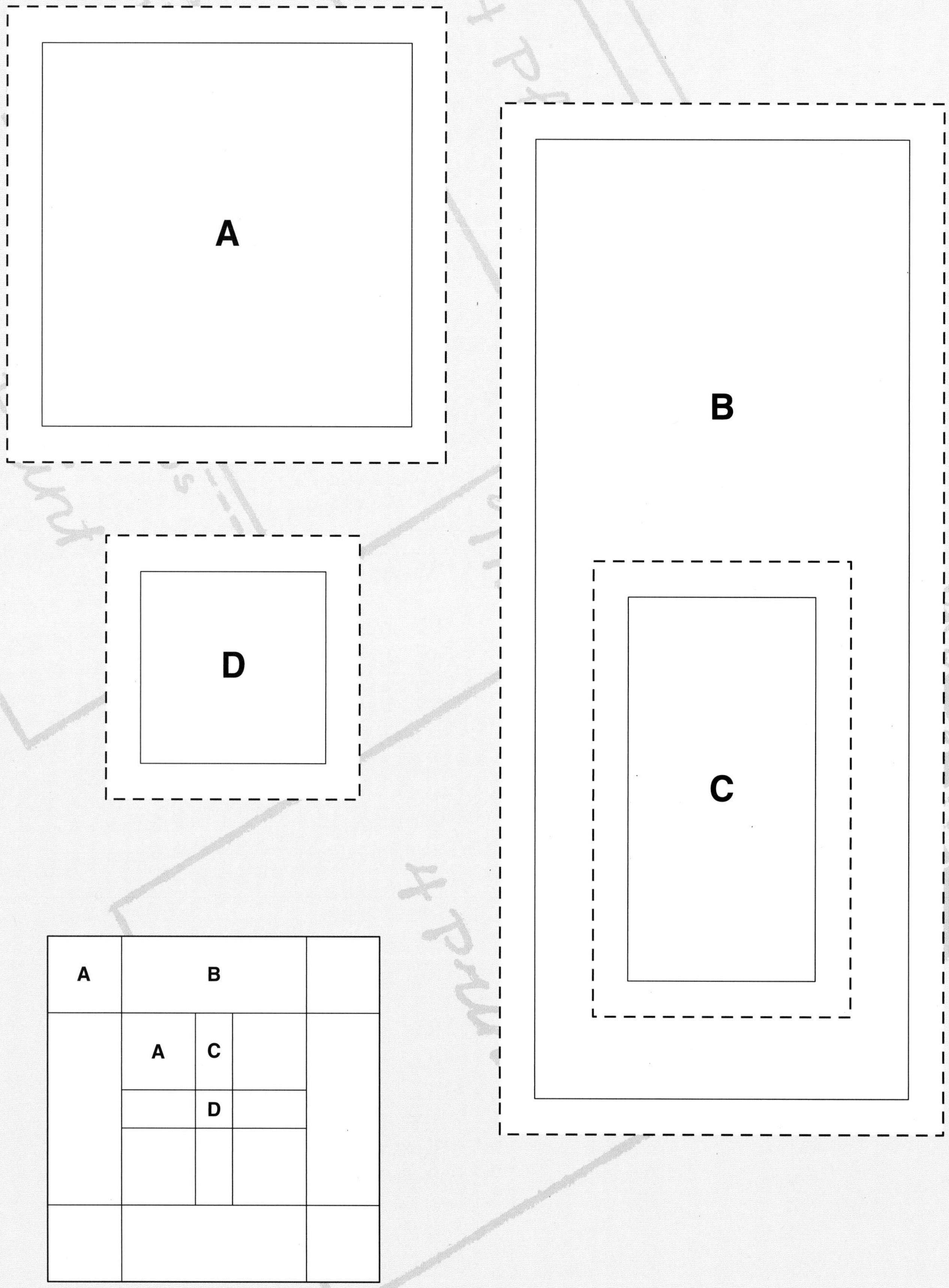

A

B

D

C

A	B	
A	C	
	D	

The Comfort Quilt

"Comfort" is an old-fashioned term for a tied comforter or coverlet. The contributor, Mrs. David Lintner of Keswick, Iowa, had a "comfort top" in this design. She probably meant a patchwork top that she planned to tie with yarn knots rather than quilt. On the other hand, this 9-Patch design could have been drafted from an old woven coverlet. The combination of squares and rectangles is simple enough for beginning quilt makers to piece, but shading and setting can create complex designs. In the 1940 pattern, *Star* columnist Edna Marie Dunn indicated the fabrics to be cut as "print" or "plain," a popular way to pair colors. Mid-century quilters loved to contrast pastel prints with pastel solid fabrics. A true light/dark contrast was not nearly as important to them as it is to us today. For a retro look, think in terms of prints vs. plains or bring the pattern up to date with sharp contrast between darks and lights.

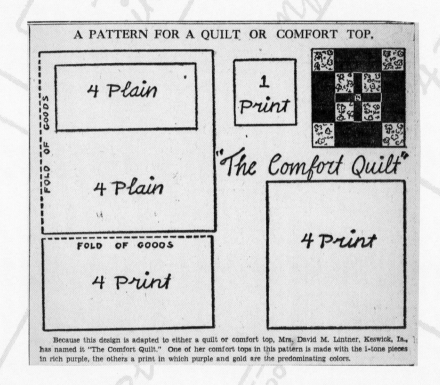

A PATTERN FOR A QUILT OR COMFORT TOP.

4 Plain

4 Plain

FOLD OF GOODS

4 Print

1 Print

"The Comfort Quilt"

4 Print

Because this design is adapted to either a quilt or comfort top, Mrs. David M. Lintner, Keswick, Ia., has named it "The Comfort Quilt." One of her comfort tops in this pattern is made with the 1-tone pieces in rich purple, the others a print in which purple and gold are the predominating colors.

The Comfort Quilt

1940

12" PATTERN

A Cut 8 light
Rotary cut 3-1/8" squares

B Cut 4 dark
Rotary cut rectangles 7-1/8" x 3-1/8"

C Cut 4 dark
Rotary cut rectangles 3-1/8" x 1-7/8"

D Cut 1 light
Rotary cut 1-7/8" square

The Little Cedar Tree
1940
12" PATTERN

A
Cut 4 light
Cut 4 dark
Rotary Cut squares 6-7/8"
Then cut into 2 triangles

A

The Little Cedar Tree

The right-angle triangle, what quilters today often call a sawtooth triangle, is the basis of many traditional patchwork designs. In 1940, a reader from Leslie, Mo., mailed a simple 4-Patch block made of eight triangles to Star pattern editor Edna Marie Dunn, who drew it for the column. When placed on point and shaded in darks and lights, the triangles form a simple tree, a shape Mrs. William Rosendahl interpreted as a cedar, a tree that thrives on the prairies near Kansas City. The pattern here is for a 12" block, which means the triangles make squares finishing to 6". Challenge rules permit you to redraft the designs any size, so you might want to use triangle papers or other fast methods available today and turn your sewing machine into a triangle assembly line.

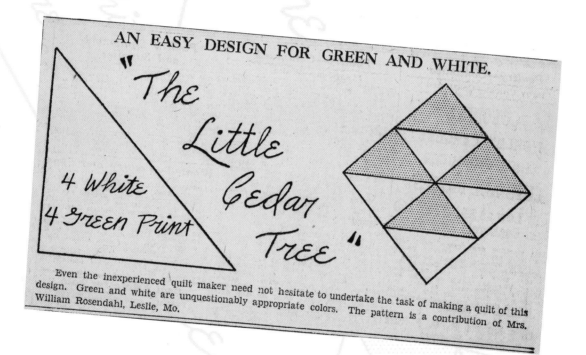

AN EASY DESIGN FOR GREEN AND WHITE.

"The Little Cedar Tree"

4 White
4 Green Print

Even the inexperienced quilt maker need not hesitate to undertake the task of making a quilt of this design. Green and white are unquestionably appropriate colors. The pattern is a contribution of Mrs. William Rosendahl, Leslie, Mo.

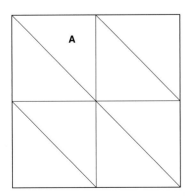

A

The Maple Leaf
1930
12" PATTERN

A Cut 4 light
  Cut 13 dark
  Rotary Cut 2-1/4" squares
B Cut 16 dark
  Cut 16 light
  Rotary Cut 2-5/8" squares
  Cut each into 2 triangles
C Cut 4 light
  Rotary Cut rectangles 5-5/8" x 2-1/4"
D Cut 8 light
  Rotary Cut 2" squares
  Cut each into 2 triangles
E Cut 4 dark

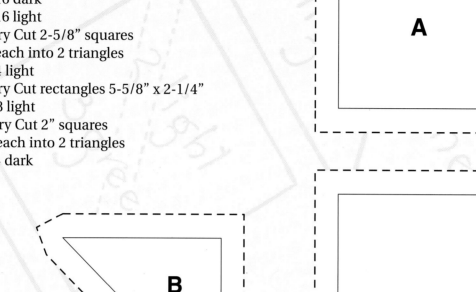

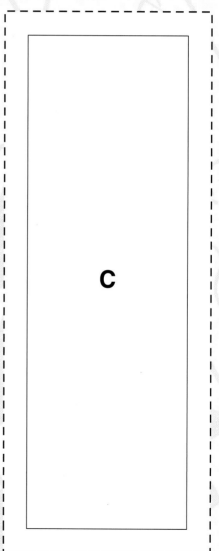

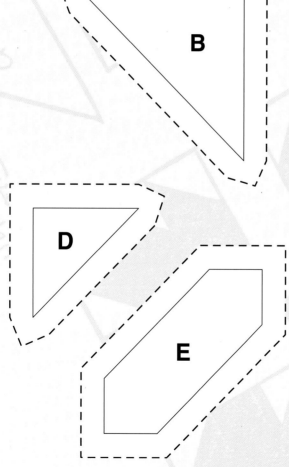

The Maple Leaf

This 9-Patch of pieced leaves is a classic 20th-century design. Eveline Foland, designing for *The Star*, thought green and white appropriate colors, but, following the emerging color trends of the 1930s, she believed a mix of pastels would be effective, too. Other color ideas were suggested by Ruby McKim, who included the block in her syndicated pattern series "The Patchwork Parade of States," calling it Autumn Leaves. Carrie Hall in her 1935 book also saw the design as Autumn Leaf. Pattern directions include rotary cutting for all pieces except the stems, piece E, which might be best cut using the template. For a 12" pattern the triangles finish out to a bit less than 2". But remember that Challenge rules say blocks can be any size, so today's quilters might find it easier to use 2" or 3" triangle papers, redrafting squares, rectangles and stems to fit.

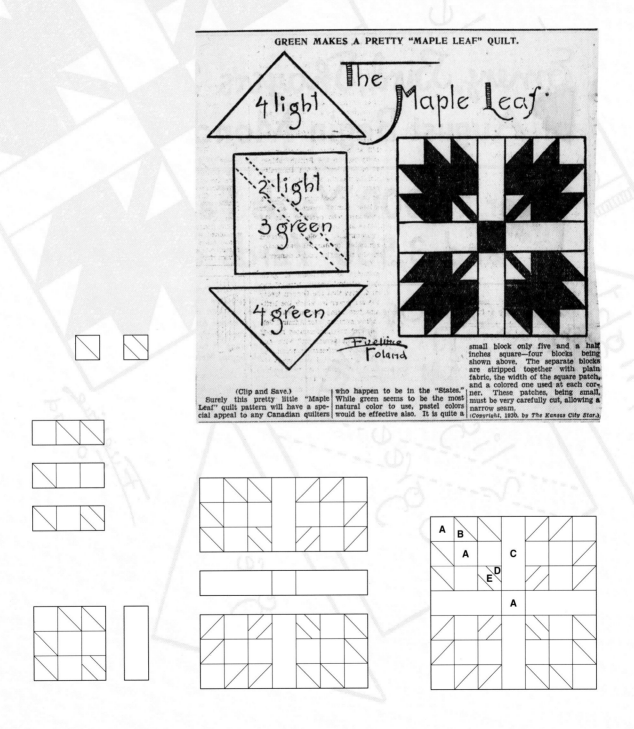

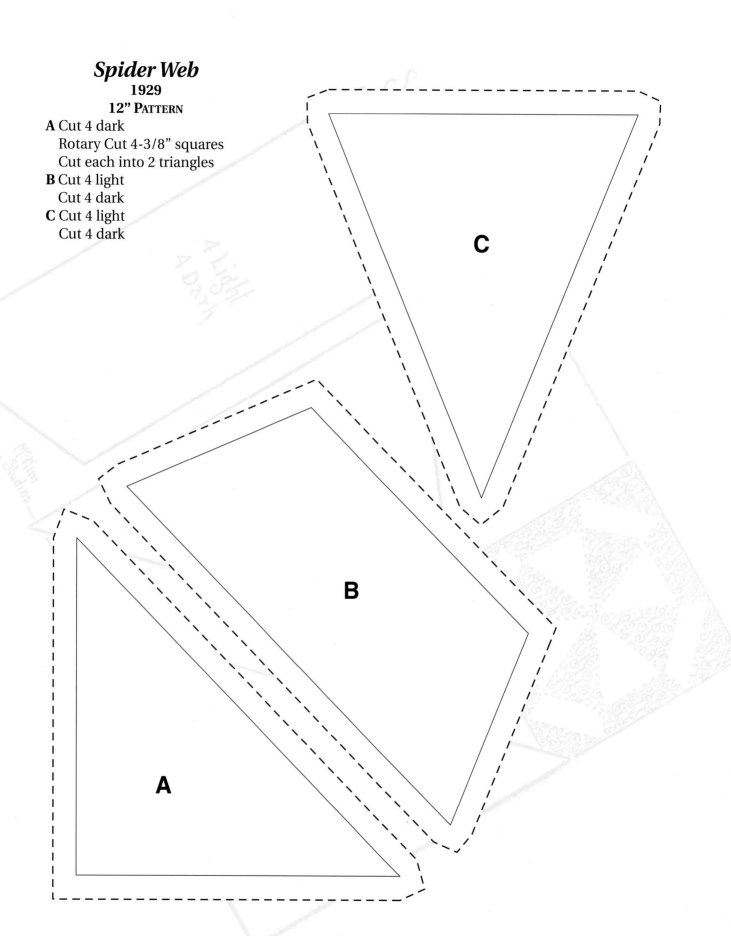

Spider Web
1929
12" Pattern
A Cut 4 dark
 Rotary Cut 4-3/8" squares
 Cut each into 2 triangles
B Cut 4 light
 Cut 4 dark
C Cut 4 light
 Cut 4 dark

C

B

A

Spider Web

Ruby McKim drew this block for the *The Star* in January 1929, advising readers to choose odd materials for a scrappy look or, perhaps, a limited color scheme of darks and lights. "Any quilt is more sophisticated made in a definite and limited color scheme," was her opinion. The corner triangles can be easily cut with a rotary cutter, but the instructions give templates only for pieces B and C. The block is one of a variety of kaleidoscopic designs that fit an octagonal shape neatly into a square block. Other published names include Denver and Boston Pavement from early 20th-century magazines. *Capper's Weekly* in Topeka saw Autumn Leaves in the design.

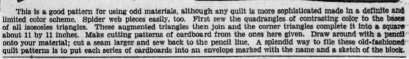

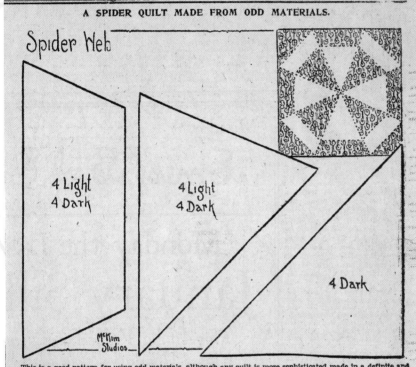

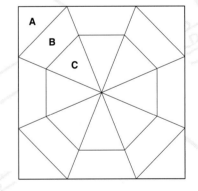

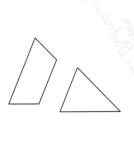

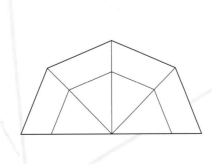

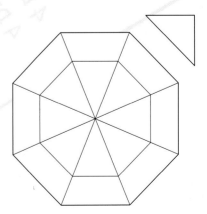

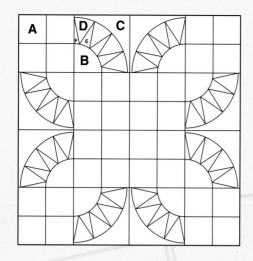

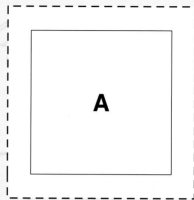

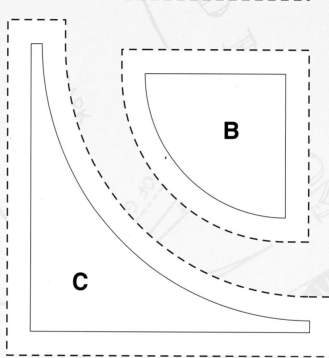

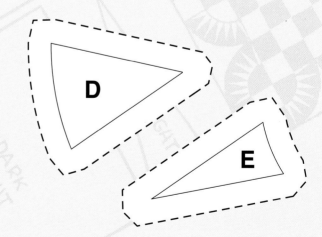

Dogwood Blossom
1934
12" PATTERN

A Cut 1 dark
  Cut 16 light
  Rotary Cut 2" squares
B Cut 4 dark
  Cut 4 light
C Cut 8 light
D Cut 32 light
E Cut 24 light
F Cut 4 light
  Flip pattern over and cut 4 more

Dogwood Blossom

Edna Marie Dunn described this block as an "intricate pattern ... to be tried only by the experienced." We've modified her version to give you fewer spikes in the arcs (5 vs. 7) and redrafted the arc for machine piecing over a paper foundation. If you want to paper piece the pattern instead of cutting pieces D, E and F, photocopy the arc 8 times. Use the templates to cut B and C and rotary cut piece A. After paper piecing the arc but before removing the paper foundation, use conventional piecing to stitch it to pieces B and C. Remove the paper foundations and piece these small patches to the checkerboards made of piece A. The design first appeared in print as Dogwood Blossom in 1928 in Topeka's *Capper's Weekly* quilt column. Other names include Suspension Bridge from Mrs. Danner's patterns in El Dorado, Kan., and Oklahoma Dogwood from the Mountain Mist batting company.

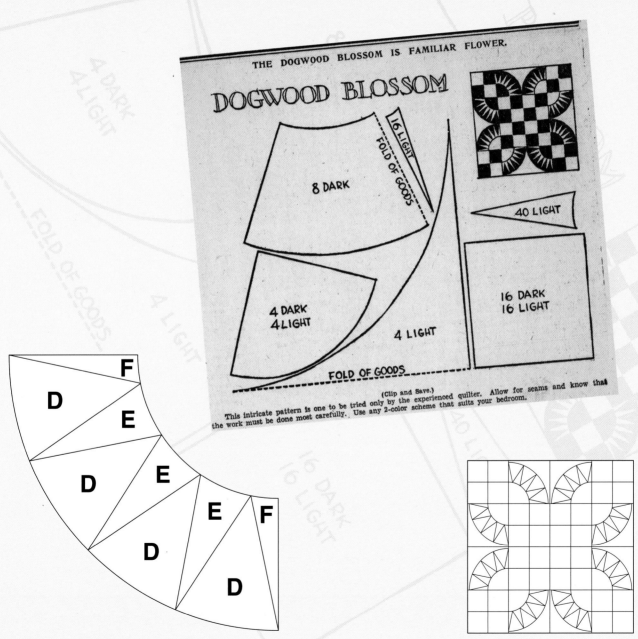

Use this foundation for paper piecing.
Photocopy it 8 times.
You have permission to photocopy this page for your own personal use.

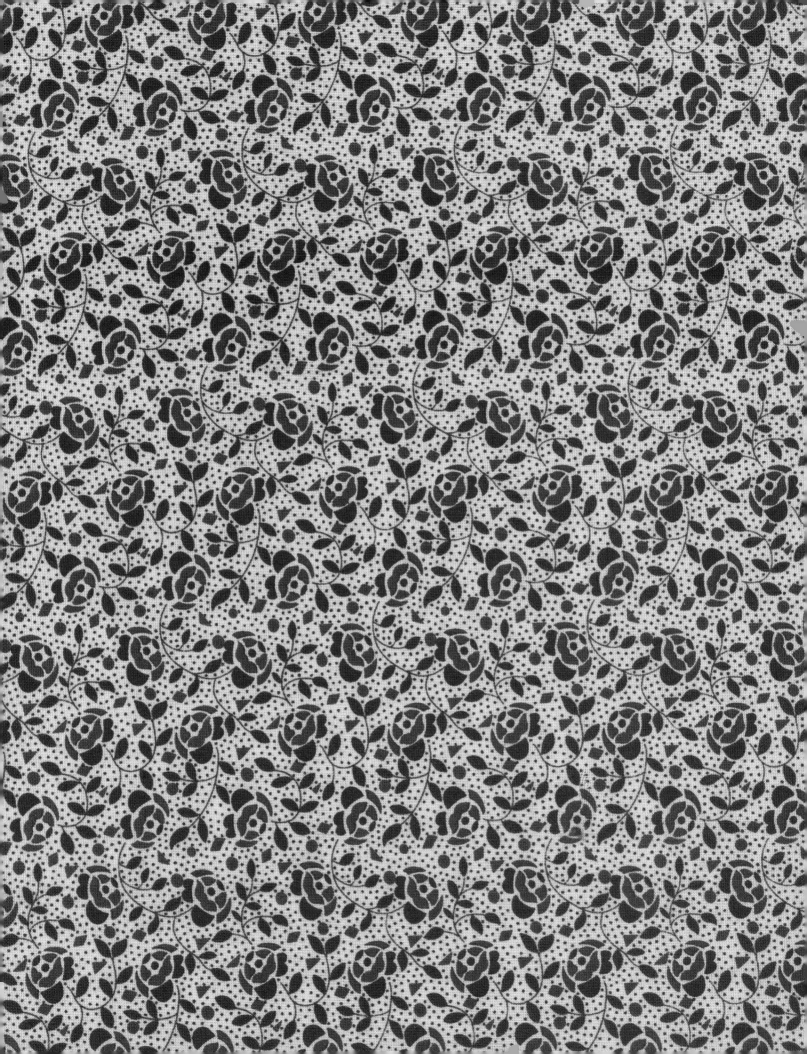

The Quilts

Through the Window

36" x 36"
By Patricia Beck of Chicora, Pa.

20

Patricia created a most innovative design by skewing the blocks, giving the quilt the appearance of depth. In essence it has only three blocks. You will make one center block and four each of the side and corner blocks.

FABRIC REQUIREMENTS

1/8 yard green solid (side blocks)
1/4 yard green with white print (corner blocks)
1/4 yard yellow with white print (side blocks)
1/8 yard white with yellow print (center block)
1/8 yard white with green print (center block)
5/8 yard green with yellow and red large floral print (corner blocks and center block)
1/3 yard yellow with red and pink large floral print (side blocks)
1/3 yard green with white and yellow print (side blocks)
1/3 yard yellow with white and green print (corner blocks)
1/8 yard yellow solid (corner blocks and center block)
1/3 yard red solid (center block and binding)
backing fabric

CUTTING INSTRUCTIONS

This is one quilt you will have to make from the templates on the following pages. Make an individual template for each piece of each block; these have been labeled for you. The side blocks use some of the templates in reverse. You may stack the fabric by folding the wrong sides together and cutting the reverse templates at the same time.

Cut your template of paper or template plastic. Place on the layered fabric and very carefully lay your rotary cutting ruler over. As long as the template is completely under the ruler, you can successfully rotary cut fabric. Cut all 4 of each template at once.

PIECING INSTRUCTIONS

While this quilt may appear to be complicated, you may find it is one of the simplest to construct. Refer to the layout model for placement and construct the blocks as you would a familiar 9-Patch block: 3 rows of 3 pieces each.

QUILTING

Patricia backed her quilt with the same floral print she used in the large pieces of the corner blocks. She did, however, reverse the fabric so that the "wrong" side was out. You know, you pay for both sides of the fabric; you should feel free to use both sides!

Patricia machine quilted her work from the reverse side. She outlined the large flowers with quilting. On the front, these lovely flowers cover the whole quilt and appear to be randomly placed.

BINDING

Refer to the instructions beginning on page 121 for directions on straight mitered binding.

The label is your final step.

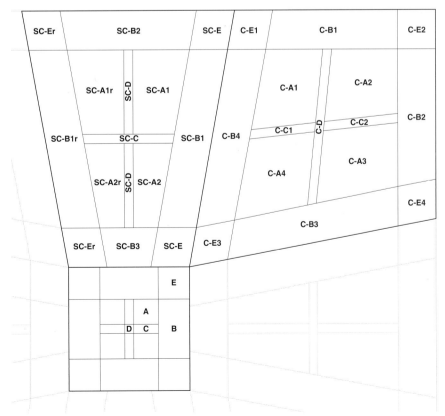

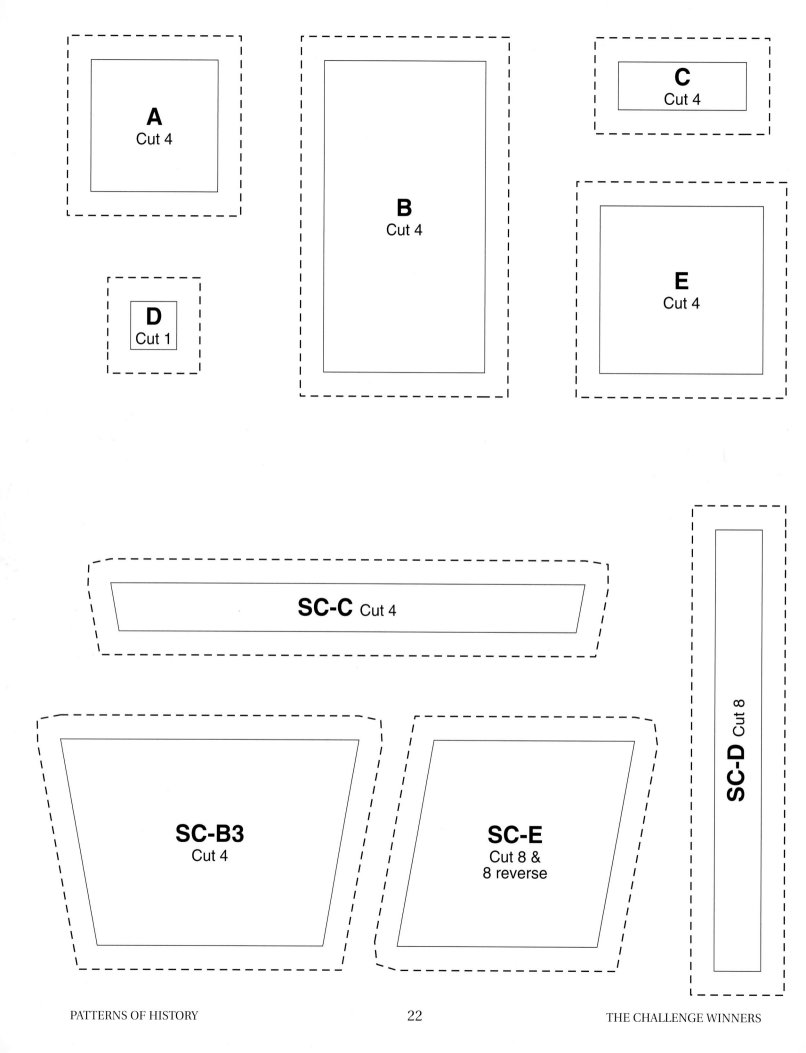

A
Cut 4

B
Cut 4

C
Cut 4

D
Cut 1

E
Cut 4

SC-C Cut 4

SC-D Cut 8

SC-B3
Cut 4

SC-E
Cut 8 &
8 reverse

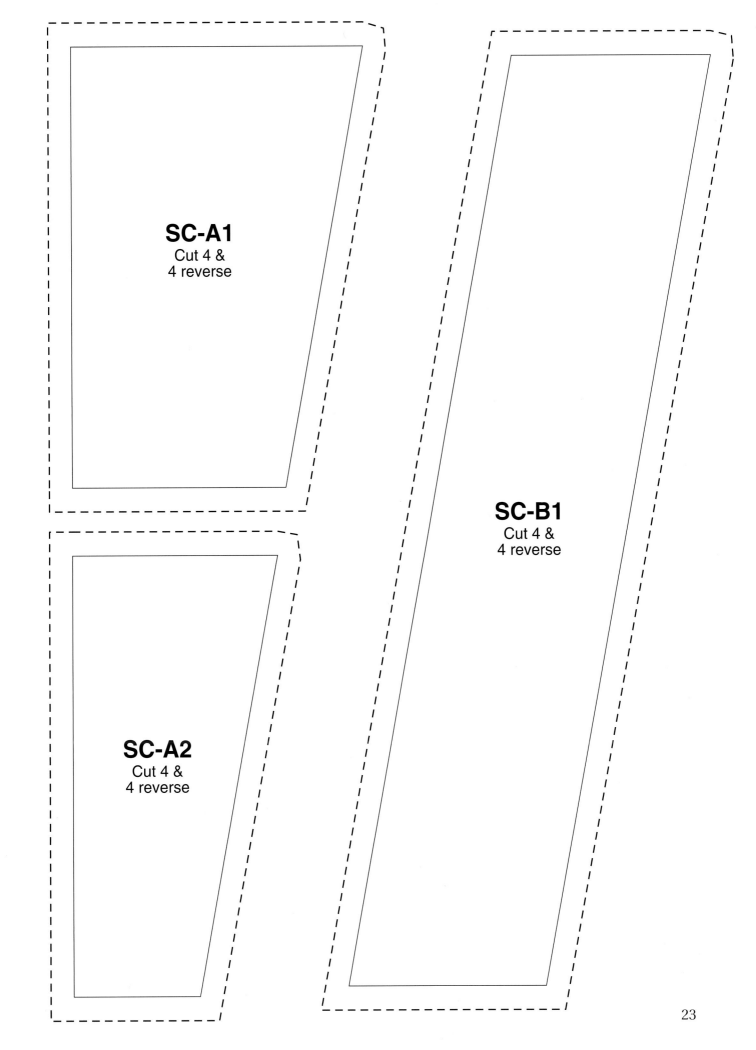

SC-A1
Cut 4 &
4 reverse

SC-B1
Cut 4 &
4 reverse

SC-A2
Cut 4 &
4 reverse

23

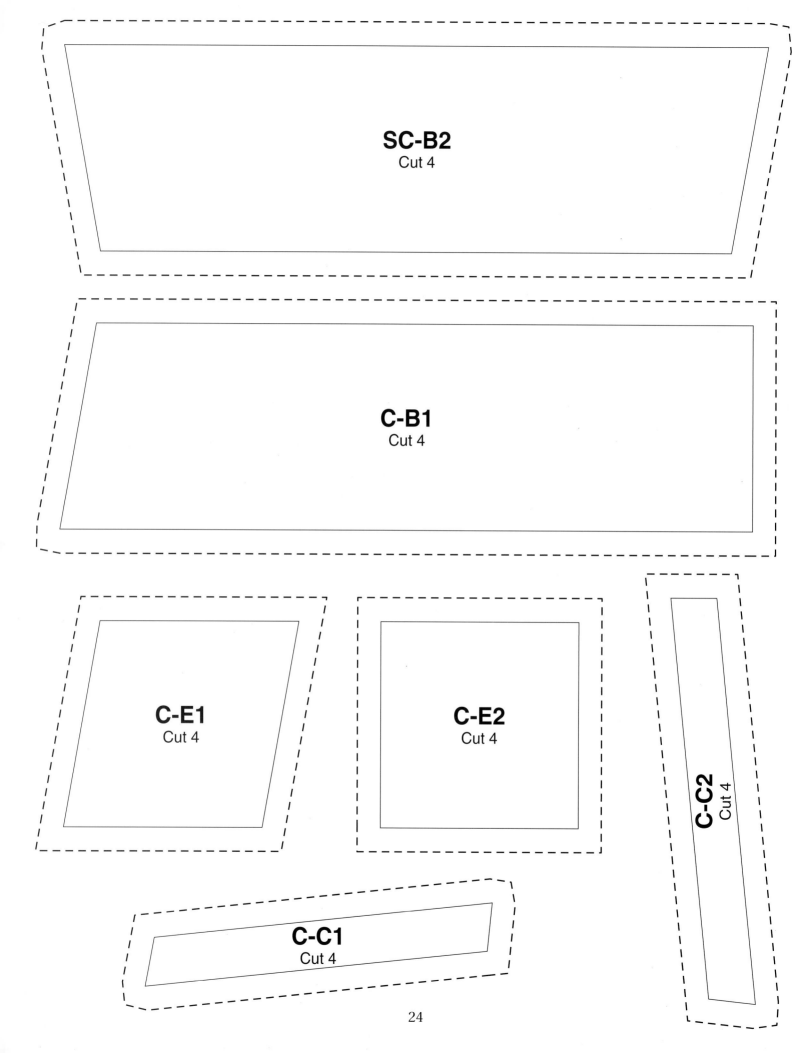

SC-B2
Cut 4

C-B1
Cut 4

C-E1
Cut 4

C-E2
Cut 4

C-C2
Cut 4

C-C1
Cut 4

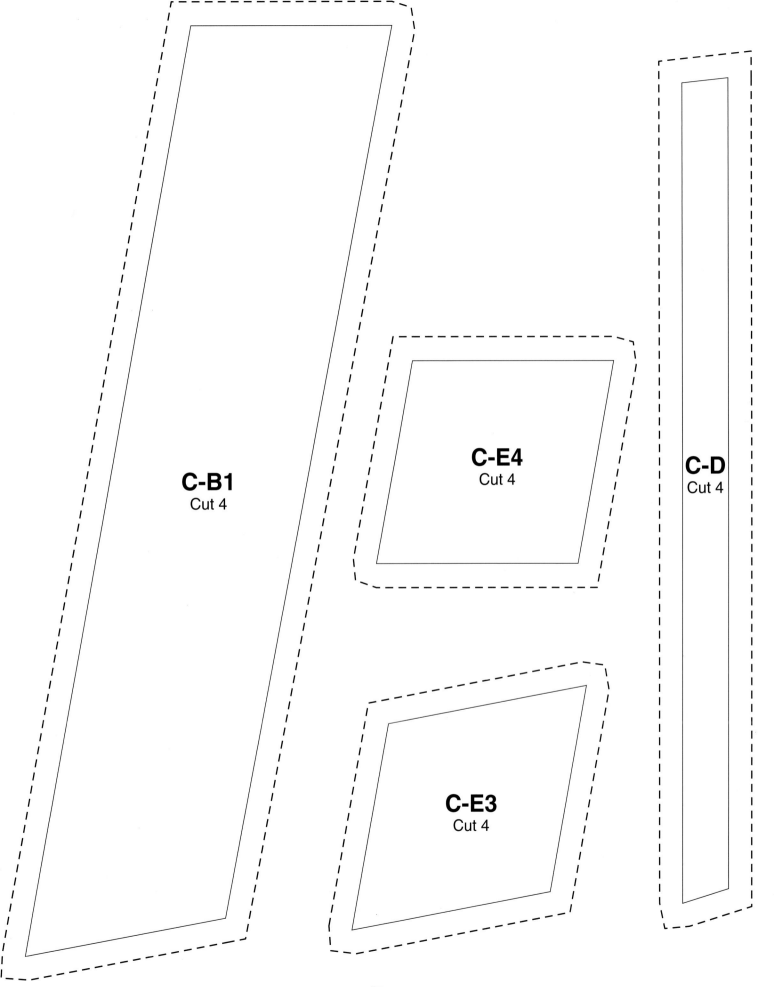

C-B1
Cut 4

C-E4
Cut 4

C-D
Cut 4

C-E3
Cut 4

THE CHALLENGE WINNERS

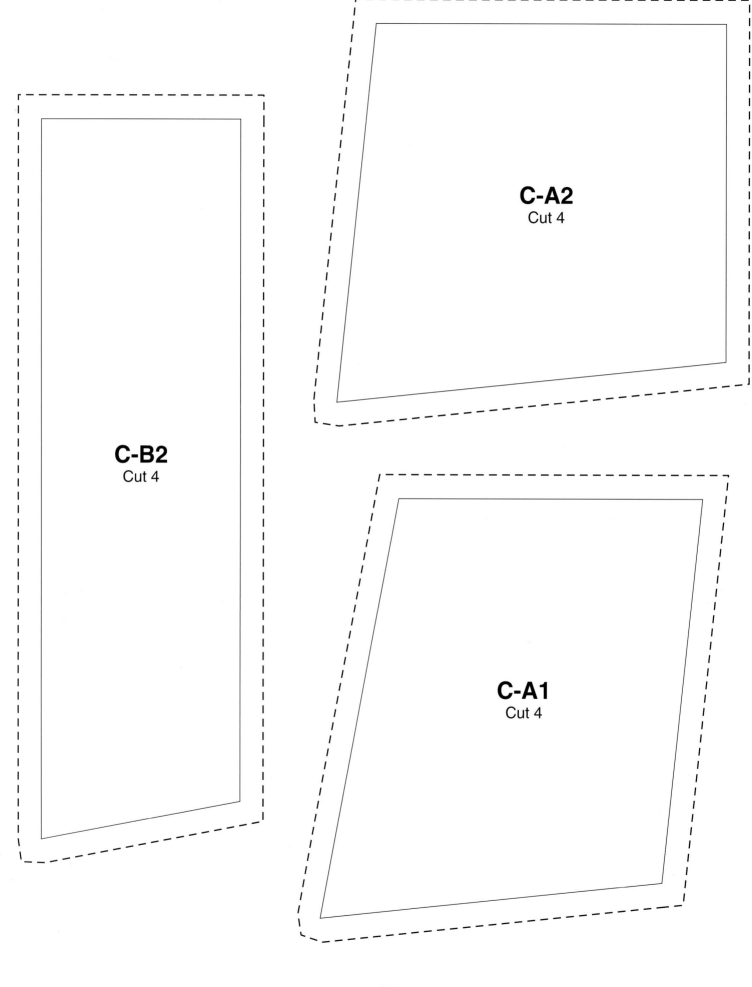

C-B2
Cut 4

C-A2
Cut 4

C-A1
Cut 4

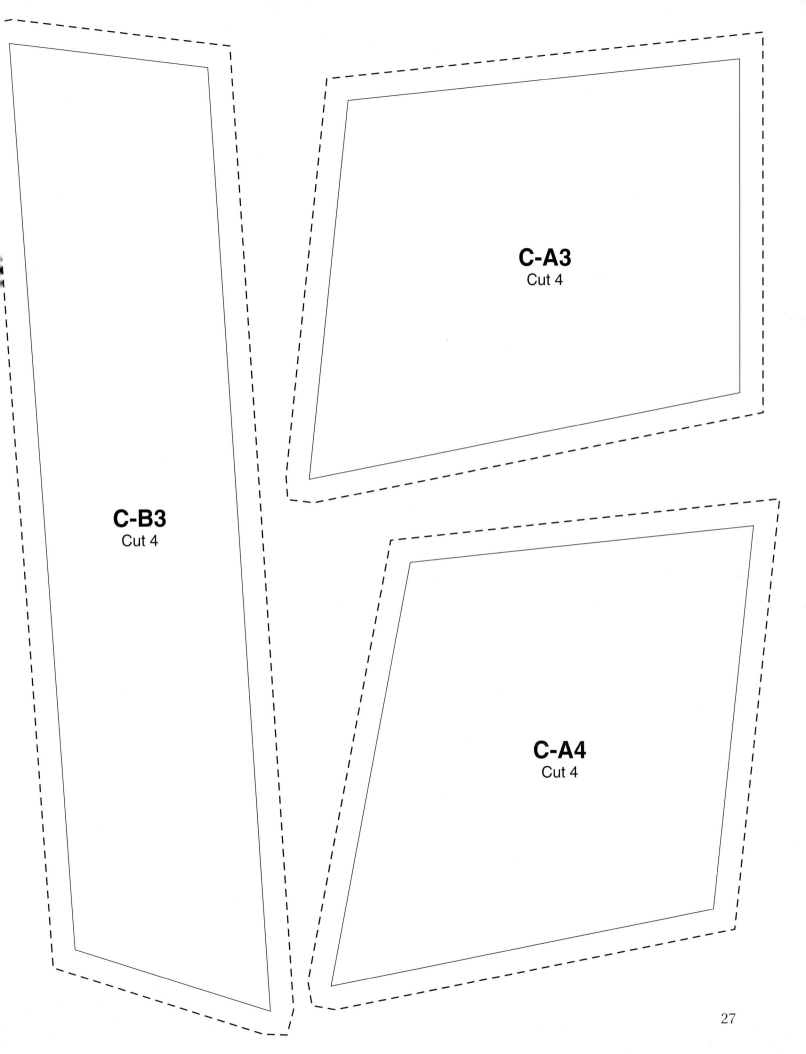

C-A3
Cut 4

C-B3
Cut 4

C-A4
Cut 4

27

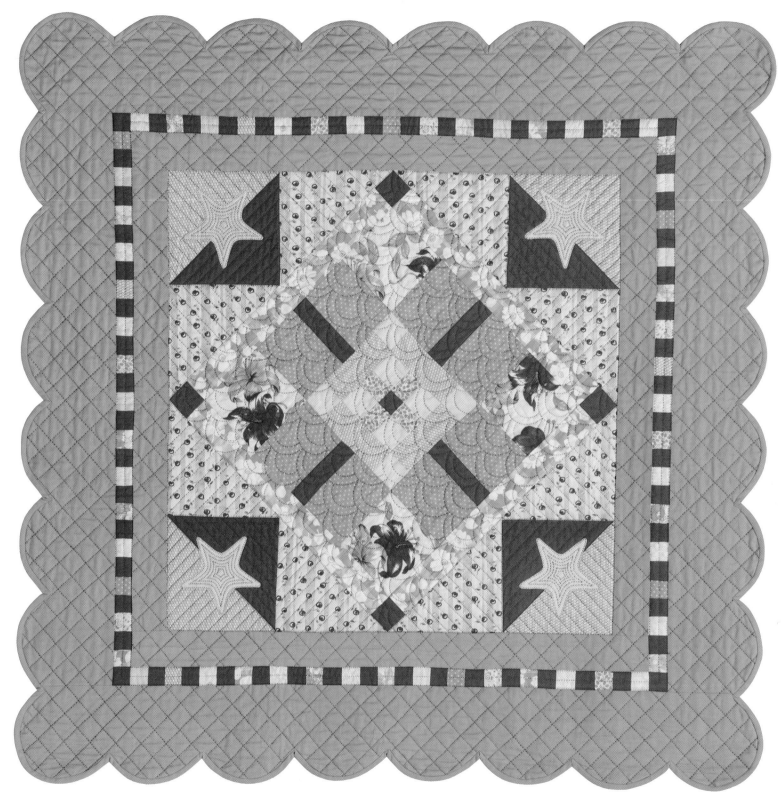

My Grandmother's Kitchen

40" x 40"
By Patricia Heath of Evergreen, Colo.

Patricia's quilt makes us all think of our Grandmother's kitchen. The charming combination of prints and Patricia's quiltmaking skills make this a delightful quilt.

FABRIC REQUIREMENTS

3/8 yard solid red (Comfort Quilt block, block frames, triangle units, outer border #2)

1/4 yard solid yellow (Comfort Quilt block, appliqué stars)

1/8 yard white with green and yellow print (Comfort Quilt block)

1/3 yard green with white and yellow print (Comfort Quilt block, triangle units)

1/4 yard green with white print (block frame #1)

1/4 yard yellow with red and pink floral (block frame #1)

1/4 yard green with white and yellow floral (block frame #2)

1/4 yard pink and white with red stripe (triangle units)

1 1/4 yards green solid (outer border #1, scalloped border, binding)

1 1/4 yards for backing (if your fabric is less than 44" wide you may have to get a little more and piece the back)

CUTTING INSTRUCTIONS

Red solid: Cut (4) 1 1/2" strips; subcut (61) 1 1/2" squares and (4) 1 1/2" x 4 1/2" rectangles. Cut (2) 7 1/2" squares. Cut (4) 2" squares.

Yellow solid: Cut (1) 2" strip; subcut (8) 2" squares.

White with green and yellow print: Cut (1) 2" strip; subcut (4) 1 1/2" x 2" rectangles.

Green with white and yellow print: Cut (1) 2" strip; subcut (4) 2" x 4 1/2" rectangles. Cut (2) 7 1/2" squares.

Green with white print: Cut (1) 3 1/2" strip; subcut (8) 3 1/2 x 4 1/2" rectangles.

Yellow with red and pink floral: Cut (4) 4 1/2" squares.

Green with white and yellow floral: Cut (2) 2" strips; reserve until center of quilt top is complete.

Pink and white with red stripe: Cut (4) 7 1/2" squares.

Refer to instructions for constructing the Comfort Quilt blocks on page 110. You will be making 1 block for this quilt, measuring 7 1/2" square (7" finished) if you sew an accurate 1/4" seam allowance.

COMFORT QUILT BLOCK FRAMES

Sew (2) 3 1/2" x 4 1/2" green with white rectangles to either side of the (4) 1 1/2" x 4 1/2" rectangle pieces. Press the seam allowances toward the green fabric pieces.

Sew 1 of these units to each side of the Comfort Quilt block. Press the seam allowance toward the added unit.

Sew a 4 1/2" yellow with red and pink square to both ends of the remaining green and red units, pressing the seam allowance toward the green fabric. Sew these new units to the top and bottom of the Comfort Quilt block, forming the first frame around the Comfort Quilt block.

The second frame is a simple strip with corner blocks. Measure through the center of your quilt top. Cut 4 pieces from the 2" green with white and yellow floral strips that you have already cut. Sew 2 of these strips to the sides of your quilt top, pressing the seam allowance toward the strip. Sew (2) 2" red solid squares to the ends of the remaining 2 strips, pressing the seam allowance toward the strips. Sew these units to the top and bottom of the quilt top.

TRIANGLE UNITS

To turn the quilt top "on point," Patricia added triangle units to the sides. This created new corners and changed the orientation of the quilt top.

Begin by pairing the solid red 7 1/2" squares each with a green with white and yellow print 7 1/2" square, right sides together. Draw a line diagonally from corner to corner on the wrong side of the lighter fabric. Sew 1/4" from the line on both sides.

Cut the squares in half on the drawn line. Press the unit open, pressing the seam allowance toward the solid red half.

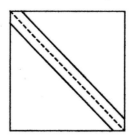

**Star for
My Grandmother's Kitchen**

**Dogwood Blossom templates for
Dogwood Festival**

Add 1/4" seam allowance to fabric

Trace the star appliqué shapes on page 30 onto the non-shiny side of freezer paper and cut them out on the drawn line. Iron the star-shaped templates onto the right side of the yellow solid fabric, leaving at least 1/2" between the paper templates. Using a marker that shows on the yellow fabric, trace around the freezer paper, right next to the template. Cut the star shapes out, adding 3/16" seam allowance.

Refer to the photograph of Patricia's quilt and place a star in the center of each of the red and green half-square triangle units. Needle-turn the seam allowance and stitch the stars in place. Once the stitching is complete, use your rotary cutter to trim the blocks to 6 3/4" square.

Cut each of the pink and white with red striped squares in half, diagonally, giving you 8 half-square triangles. (I have deliberately made these triangles oversized.) Sew a triangle to each of the red edges of the half-square triangle units, matching the corners. The pink triangles will overlap at the bias edges.

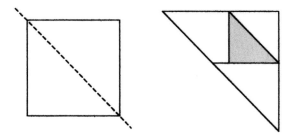

Just before sewing the triangle units to the side of the quilt top, trim the bias edge, leaving 1/4" seam allowance.

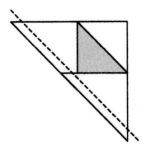

When you sew the triangle to the quilt top, place the triangle unit against the throat plate and the quilt top on top. This will let the feed dogs ease the fabric as you sew the seam. If the triangle unit is on top, the foot will cause the bias edge to stretch. Pressing the seam allowance away from the triangle unit will ease the bulk where the 2 triangles and the appliquéd square come together.

BORDERS

The first border is a simple border using the green solid fabric. Cut (4) 2 1/2" strips from the solid green fabric. Measure through the vertical center of the quilt top and trim 2 of the strips to that measurement. Sew the strips to the sides of the quilt top. Press the seam allowanced toward the border strips.

Measure through the horizontal middle of the quilt top and trim the 2 remaining strips to that length. Sew the strips to the top and bottom of the quilt top. Press the seam allowances toward the borders strips.

Trim the quilt top at this point so it measures 29 1/2" on each side. It must measure exactly 29 1/2" square for the next border to fit.

The second border is made up of squares, half cut from the red solid and half from a variety of prints, both from the quilt itself and from fabrics that coordinate closely. You need a total of (60) 1 1/2" squares from a variety of fabrics and (60) 1 1/2" squares from the solid red fabric.

Sew 4 strips from the squares. Sew 2 strips by alternating a print with the red, a total of 29 squares, beginning and ending with a print square. Sew 2 strips by alternating a print with a red, a total of 31 squares, beginning and ending with a red solid square.

Sew the shorter strips to the sides of the quilt top. Press the seam allowance toward the first border. Sew the longer strips to the top and bottom of the quilt top. Press the seam allowance toward the first border.

Cut (4) 5" strips from the green solid fabric. Measure the vertical center of the quilt top and cut 2 of the strips that length. Sew the strips to the sides of the quilt top. Measure through the horizontal middle of the quilt top and cut the remaining 2 strips that length. Sew the strips to the top and bottom of the quilt top.

Refer to the technique pages near the end of the book for directions for a scalloped edge.

QUILTING

Patricia hand quilted her design. If you study the photograph of her quilt, you will see that she combined a traditional sashiko design with channel quilting and grid quilting. I love the red thread she used!

BINDING

Refer to page 125 for directions on binding a scalloped edge.

Don't forget to make a label for your quilt!

Blue Dogwood Trail

40 1/2" x 60 1/2"

By Peggy Thackston of San Antonio, Texas

Peggy's quilt is quite distinctive.
She made half the arcs with dark spikes and light background and half with light
spikes and dark background. The combination created a secondary design
that gives the impression that Dogwood Blossoms have thorns!

Refer to the Dogwood Blossom block pattern on page 114. You will need to make templates for B and C. You will need 160 copies of the foundation for paper piecing. Piece A will be rotary cut and strip pieced according to the directions on page 113.

FABRIC REQUIREMENTS
3 7/8 yards blue (includes binding)
6 3/8 yards cream and blue background
2 3/4 yards for backing

BLOCK CONSTRUCTION
4-Patch Units
This quilt has (160) 4-Patch units. Begin by making strip sets.
Blue: Cut (16) 2" strips from selvage to selvage.
Cream and blue background: Cut (16) 2" strips from selvage to selvage.

Sew the blue strips each to a cream and blue background strip, along the long edge, and press the seam allowance toward the blue print. You should have 16 strip sets that measure 3 1/2" wide.

Crosscut the strips into segments that are 2" x 3 1/2". You need a total of 320 segments.

Construct the 4-Patch units by pairing two segments, alternating dark and light. You will make (160) 4-Patch units.

Arcs
You will be making 160 arcs. Eighty arcs will have dark spikes on a light background and light template B pieces, and 80 will have light spikes on a dark background with dark template B pieces. All 160 arc units will have light template C pieces. Refer to page XX for paper foundation piecing instructions.

Blue fabric: Cut (16) 2 1/2" strips; subcut to (320) 2" x 2 1/2" rectangles for the background of the cream and blue spikes. Cut (10) 2 1/2" strips; subcut to (400) 1" x 2 1/2" rectangles for spikes. Cut 80 B template pieces.
Cream and blue fabric: Cut (10) 2 1/2" strips; subcut to (400) 1" x 2 1/2" rectangles for spikes. Cut (16) 2 1/2" strips; subcut to (320) 2" x 2 1/2" rectangles for the background to the blue spikes. Cut 80 B template pieces. Cut 160 C template pieces.

Once you have each of the arcs paper foundation pieced, you will add the B and C template pieces. Sew a blue B template piece to each of the arcs that have cream and blue spikes and blue background. Sew a cream and blue B template piece to each of the arcs with blue spikes and cream and blue backgrounds. Sew the cream and blue template C pieces to each of the 160 arcs.

Each of the 20 blocks in this quilt is made by combining (8) 4-Patch units, 4 arc units with blue spikes and 4 arc units with cream and blue spikes. Refer to the photograph below of the block and arrange the units. I find it best to sew the block together in quarters and then sew the quarters together. Remember to press the seam allowances in opposite directions. This will let your block lie flatter.

When sewing the blocks together, be sure they are all oriented the same way. Sew the blocks together in 5 rows of 4 blocks each, then sew the rows together.

QUILTING
Peggy machine quilted "in the ditch" between each of the 3 1/2" units, creating a grid over the entire surface.

BINDING
Peggy chose to let the blocks run all the way to the edge. She added no border, instead letting the binding act as a border to stop your eye. She used the blue fabric for the binding.

Cut (6) 2 1/2" strips from the blue fabric. Following the instructions in the techniques section near the end of the book for binding a straight edge, finish your quilt.

Don't forget to add a label to document your work.

Dogwood Reflections

61" x 73"
Made by Kathryn Botsford of Campbell River, British Columbia

Kathryn decided to work with both traditional blocks and ones she tweaked by replacing three 4-Patch units with arcs in the blocks in the four corners and two 4-Patch units with arcs in the blocks around the outside edge. This gives her quilt the appearance of floating over a light background. The scalloped edge of the border continues the motif. Notice, too, that Kathryn created a secondary design by paying attention to her color and value placement.

Refer to the Dogwood Blossom block pattern on page 16. You will need to make templates for B and C. You will need 191 copies of the foundation for paper piecing. Piece A will be rotary cut and strip pieced according to the instructions beginning on page 113.

FABRIC REQUIREMENTS

5/8 yard solid red (spike background in arc)
5/8 yard solid blue (spike background in arc)
2 1/4 yards red print #1 (spike background in arc, arc outer corners, inner border #1 and binding)
3/8 yard red print #2 (4-Patch units, arc inner corners)
3/8 yard red print #3 (4-Patch units, arc inner corners)
3/4 yard red print #4 (arc outside corners)
1/3 yard red print #5 (inner border #2)
1 1/4 yards blue print #1 (spike background in arc)
1/3 yard blue print #2 (4-Patch units)
1/3 yard blue print #3 (4-Patch units)
1/2 yard blue print #4 (arc inside corners)
3 yards cream and red background print (spike in arc, 4-Patch units, arc inside corners, arc outside corners)
3 3/8 yards cream and blue background print (spike in arc, 4-Patch units, arc inside corners, arc outside corners)
3 7/8 yards cream/red/blue border print (arc outside corners, outside scalloped border)
4 1/8 yards backing fabric

BLOCK CONSTRUCTION

Each traditional Dogwood Blossom block (Block A) is made from 8 arc units and (8) 4-Patch units. Kathryn also made two variations on the Dogwood Blossom block (Block B and Block C). Block B is made from 10 arc units and (6) 4-Patch units. Block C is made from 11 arc units and (5) 4-Patch units. All cutting instructions are based on rotary cutting from selvage to selvage and 40 usable inches of fabric after the selvages have been removed.

4-Patch Units

This quilt has (128) 4-Patch units, 64 made from red fabrics and 64 from blue. Placement in the blocks gives the secondary design. Begin by making strip sets.

Red print #2: Cut (4) 2" strips from selvage to selvage.
Red print #3: Cut (4) 2" strips from selvage to selvage.
Blue print #2: Cut (4) 2" strips from selvage to selvage.
Blue print #3: Cut (4) 2" strips from selvage to selvage.
Cream and red background print: Cut (8) 2" strips from selvage to selvage.

Cream and blue background print: Cut (8) 2" strips from selvage to selvage.

Sew each red print #2 strip and red print #3 strip to a cream and red background print along the long edge; press the seam allowance toward the red print. Sew the blue print #2 and the blue print #3 strips each to a cream and blue background print along the long edge; press the seam allowance toward the blue print. You should have 8 strips sets 3 1/2" wide.

Crosscut the strips into segments that are 2" x 3 1/2". You need 64 segments from each strip-set combination: 64 red #2 segments, 64 red #3 segments, 64 blue #2 segments and 64 blue #3 segments.

Construct 4-Patch units by pairing a red #2 segment with a red #3 segment. You will be making 64 red 4-Patch units.

Construct 4-Patch units by pairing a blue #2 segment with a blue #3 segment. You will be making 64 blue 4-Patch units.

Arcs

You will make 202 arcs: 100 will use the solid red, solid blue and cream and red background fabrics; 102 will use red #1, blue #1 and cream and blue background fabrics. Refer to page 119 for Paper Foundation Piecing instructions.

Solid red fabric: Cut (7) 2 1/2" strips from selvage to selvage; subcut 2" x 2 1/2" rectangles. You will need 198 rectangles for the spike background in 99 arcs.
Solid blue fabric: Cut (7) 2 1/2" strips from selvage to selvage; subcut to 2" x 2 1/2" rectangles. You will need 198 rectangles for the spike background in 99 arcs.
Cream and red background print: Cut (13) 2" strips from selvage to selvage; subcut to 1" x 2" rectangles. You will need 495 rectangles for 99 arc units.
Red print #1: Cut (6) 2 1/2" strips from selvage to selvage; subcut to 2" x 2 1/2" rectangles. You will need 184 rectangles for 92 arc units.
Blue print #1: Cut (6) 2 1/2" strips from selvage to selvage; subcut to 2" x 2 1/2" rectangles. You will need 184 rectangles for 92 arc units.
Cream and blue background print: Cut (13) 2" strips from selvage to selvage; subcut to 1" x 2" rectangles. You will need 460 rectangles for 92 arc units.
Alternate the background patches on 99 arcs between red and blue solids. The spikes are all of cream and red background fabric.

Alternate the background patches on the remaining 92 arcs between red print #1 and blue print #1. The spikes are all of cream and blue background fabric.

Template B

Red print #2: Cut 7 template B pieces. These are to be sewn to 4 arcs with solid red and blue pieces and 3 arcs with red and blue print pieces.

Red print #3: Cut 7 template B pieces. These are to be sewn to 4 arcs with solid red and blue pieces and 3 arcs with red and blue print pieces.

Blue print #4: Cut 144 template B pieces. These are to be sewn to 72 arcs with solid red and blue pieces and 72 arcs with red and blue print pieces.

Cream and red background: Cut 14 template B pieces. These are to be sewn to 14 arcs with solid red and blue pieces.

Cream and blue background: Cut 20 template B pieces. These are to be sewn to 20 arcs with red and blue print pieces.

Template C

Red print #1: Cut 30 pieces from template C. These are to sewn to 30 arcs with solid red and blue pieces with blue print #4 template B pieces.

Red print #4: Cut 30 pieces from template C. These are to be sewn to 30 arcs with solid red and blue pieces with blue print #4 template B pieces.

Cream and red background print: You will need 28 pieces from template C for the outside corner of 28 arc units; 13 have cream and red background template B pieces, 3 have red #2 template B pieces, 4 have red #3 template B pieces and 8 have blue #4 template B pieces.

Cream and blue background print: You will need 40 pieces from template C for the

outside corner of 40 arc units; 20 have cream and blue background template B pieces, 12 have blue #4 template B pieces, 4 have red #2 template B pieces and 4 have red #3 template B pieces.

Cream, red and blue border print: You will need 64 pieces from template C for the outside corner of 64 red #1 and blue #1 arc units, each with blue #4 template B pieces.

At this point, you will have 10 different arc units.

Now is the time to get your design wall cleaned off. I recommend that you study the photograph of Kathryn's quilt and start laying out arc units and 4-Patch units if you want to duplicate her secondary design. Each 12 1/2" (unfinished) block will consist of 16 units. I find that if I sew the units into 4-Patch blocks and then sew those 4-Patch blocks into the Dogwood Blossom block, the blocks seem to lie flatter. Remember to press your seams in opposite directions to aid in the construction.

Once your blocks are all constructed, sew them into rows and then sew the rows together. Press carefully – press, don't iron – and then you'll be ready for your borders. At this point, measure the quilt top. If your seams have been accurate, it may measure about 48 1/2" x 60 1/2".

BORDERS

Inner Border #1 – red print #1: Cut (6) 1 1/4" strips from selvage to selvage. Remove the selvages. From 2 strips, cut a 15" piece and sew these to 2 full strips. This will give you strips long enough for the top and bottom. Sew the remaining 25" pieces to the remaining 2 full strips. This will give you strips long enough for the sides.

Inner Border #2 – red print #5: Cut (6) 1 1/2" strips from selvage to selvage. Remove the selvages. From 2 strips, cut a 15" piece and sew these to the ends of 2 full strips. This will give you strips long enough for the top and bottom. Sew the remaining 25-inch pieces to the remaining 2 full strips for the sides.

Outer scalloped border – cream, red and blue border print: Remove selvages and cut (4) 6 1/2" strips from the length of the fabric.

Find the center of each shorter inner border strip. Align these centers and sew the strips together with a 1/4" seam allowance. Be sure to stagger the seam that connects the lengths of border strips. Press the seam allowance toward the wider strip.

Find the center of each longer inner border strip. Align these centers with strip sets and sew the strips together with a 1/4"inch seam allowance. Be sure to stagger the seam that connects the lengths of border strips. Press the seam allowance toward the narrower strip.

Find the center of each 6 1/2" border strips. Align these centers with the strip sets and sew with a 1/4" seam allowance. Press the seam allowances in the same direction as the strip set. Notice that the seam allowances alternate in direction, letting you match the corners well.

Measure through the vertical center of your quilt top. Find the center of each side and match that to the center of the side border strip sets. Measure out from the center half the measurement of the vertical center, and pin to the quilt top 1/4" from the end. Repeat with the other half. Sew the strips to the quilt top, beginning 1/4" from the end and stopping 1/4" from the other end.

Measure through the horizontal center of your quilt top. Find the center of the top and bottom of the quilt top and match that to the center of the top and bottom of the border strip sets. Measure out from the center, half the measurement of the horizontal center, and pin to the quilt top 1/4" from the end. Repeat with the other half. Sew the strips to the quilt top, beginning 1/4" from the end and stopping 1/4" from the other end.

Refer to page 121 for directions in mitered corners.

Refer to page 125 for directions in making a scalloped border.

QUILTING

Kathryn quilted Dogwood Reflections with her sewing machine, using nylon thread and stitching in the ditch between each of the 3" blocks. She also stitched in the ditch, defining the 4-Patch units in each block, and then quilted in the ditch to define the arcs. She did not quilt around each spike. In the border she quilted a series of half-circles to replicate the scallops.

BINDING

From a 5/8-yard piece of the binding fabric, cut 2 1/2" strips for the bias binding. You will need enough strips so that when they are sewn end to end they measure about 325 inches. Refer to page 125 for directions in binding a scalloped border.

Don't forget to include a label and you're finished. Now stand back and admire your beautiful quilt!

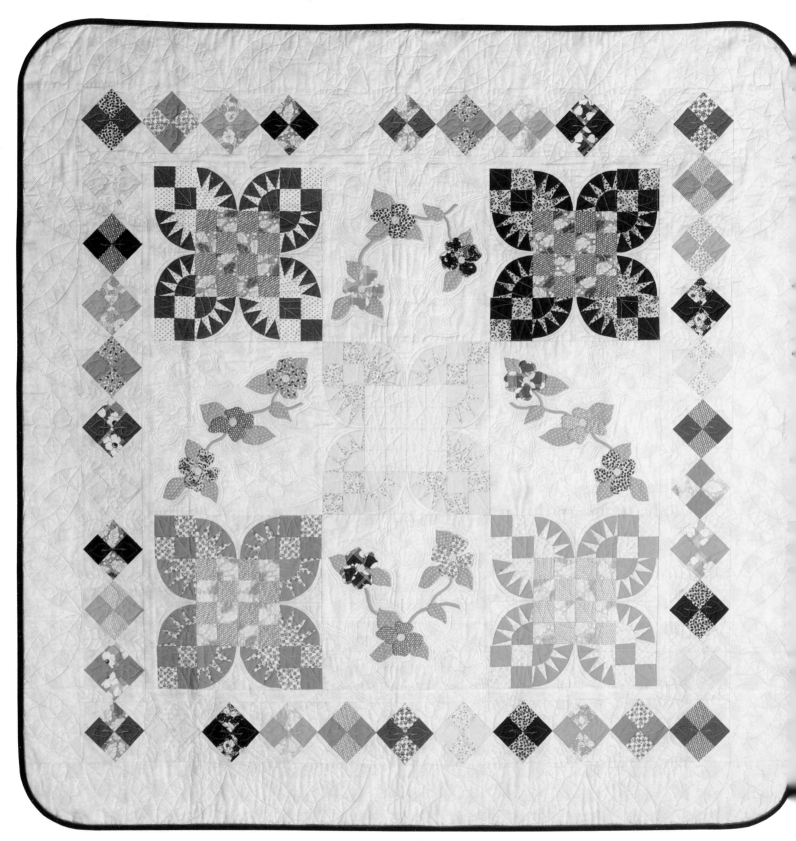

Dogwood Festival

54" x 54"
Made by Annie Brasseale of Madison, Ala.

Annie combined the Dogwood Blossom block with a Dogwood appliqué design by Edie McGinnis from her book "The Sister Blocks" (Kansas City Star Books; 2001). Annie made this cheerful quilt as a gift for her sister, Nancy.

Refer to the Dogwood Blossom pattern and templates on page 16. You will need to make templates for B and C. You will need 40 copies of the foundation for paper piecing. Piece A will be rotary cut and strip pieced following the instructions on page 113.

This is a very fat-quarter-friendly quilt!

FABRIC REQUIREMENTS

2 yards white with yellow print #1 (outer border, middle border, inner border, appliqué background, template C pieces)

1/2 yard solid red (spike background, 4-Patch units, B template pieces, piping)

Fat quarter white with red print #1(spikes, 4-Patch units, B template pieces)

Fat quarter white with red print #2 (4-Patch units)

Fat quarter red with white and blue print (4-Patch units)

1/2 yard solid dark blue (spike background, 4-Patch units, B template pieces, binding)

Fat quarter white with blue and red print (4-Patch units, B template pieces)

Fat quarter white with blue print (4-Patch units)

Fat quarter blue with white print (4-Patch units)

Fat quarter solid yellow (spike background, 4-Patch units, B template, flower centers)

Fat quarter white with yellow and green print (spikes, 4-Patch units, B template pieces)

Fat quarter yellow with white print #2 (4-Patch units)

Fat quarter yellow with white and green print (4-Patch units)

Fat quarter solid green (spike background, 4-Patch units, template B pieces)

Fat quarter white with green and yellow print (spikes, 4-Patch units, template B pieces)

Fat quarter white with green print (4-Patch units)

Fat quarter green with white print (4-Patch units)

Fat quarter solid light blue (spike background, 4-Patch units, template B pieces)

Fat quarter white with red and light blue print (spikes, 4-Patch units, template B pieces)

Fat quarter white with light blue print (4-Patch units)

Fat quarter light blue with white and red print (4-Patch units)

Fat quarter green with white print (appliqué stems and leaves)

1/8 yard assorted red, blue, and yellow prints (appliqué flowers, 4-Patch units)

3 1/3 yards (backing)

CONSTRUCTING THE UNITS

All cuts are across the grain, from selvage to selvage. That is, the strips cut from the fat quarters will be taken from the long edge. Cut an 18" piece off the 2-yard piece of white with yellow print. You will make all your cuts from this larger piece from the length of the fabric once the selvages have been removed. From the 18" piece you will be cutting across the grain, selvage to selvage.

4-Patch Units in the Dogwood Blossom Blocks

Each 4-Patch unit, when complete, should measure 3 1/2" square.

Cut the 1/2 yard of solid red fabric into 2 fat quarters and set one aside for the bias strips you will cut for the piping. Use the other fat quarter for the 4-patch unit of the red Dogwood Blossom block.

Red solid: Cut (1) 2" x 22" strip.
White with red print #1: Cut (1) 2" x 22" strips.

Sew the red strip to the white with red print strip along the long edge, right sides together. Press the seam allowance toward the red solid. Subcut the strip set into (8) 2" segments.

Pairing (2) 2" segments, invert 1 and sew them together, creating the 4-Patch block units. You will need (8) 4-Patch block for the red Dogwood Blossom block.

White with red print #2: Cut (1) 2" x 22" strip.
Red with white and blue print: Cut (1) 2" x 22" strip.

Sew the white with red print strip to the red with white and blue print strip along the long edge, right sides together. Press the seam allowance toward the red with white and blue print. Subcut the strip set into (8) 2" segments.

Pairing (2) 2" units, invert 1 and sew them together, creating the 4-Patch block units. You will need (8) 4-Patch block units to complete the red Dogwood Blossom block.

The remaining 4 Dogwood Blossom blocks are constructed in the same way as the red one, so follow the instructions for both sets of (8) 4-patch units for the dark blue, yellow, green and light blue blocks. **Press the seam allowance toward the fabric marked with an asterisk.**

Refer to the photograph to guide you.

Dark blue block

You will need (8) 4-patch units from each set of fabrics. Cut (1) 2" x 22" strip from each fabric.
   *Dark blue solid
   White with blue and red print
   White with blue print
   *Blue with white print

Yellow block

You will need (8) 4-patch units from each set of fabrics. Cut (1) 2" x 22" strip from each fabric.
   *Yellow solid
   White with yellow and green print
   *Yellow with white #2
   Yellow with white and green

Green block

You will need (8) 4-patch units from each set of fabrics. Cut (1) 2" x 22" strip from each fabric.
   *Green solid
   White with green and yellow print
   White with green print
   *Green with white print

Light blue block

You will need (8) 4-patch units from each set of fabrics. Cut (1) 2" x 22" strip from each fabric.
   *Light blue solid
   White with red and light blue print
   White with light blue print
   *Light blue with white and red print

Arc Units

Refer to page 119 for instructions on Paper Foundation Piecing. You will need 8 arcs from each of the fabric pairs listed below.

Solid red: Cut (3) 2 1/2" x 22" strips; subcut to (32) 2" x 2 1/2" rectangles.

White with red print #1: Cut (2) 2" x 22" strips; subcut to (40) 1" x 2" rectangles.

Solid dark blue: Cut (3) 2 1/2" x 22" strips; subcut to (32) 2" x 2 1/2" rectangles.

White with blue and red print: Cut (2) 2" x 22" strips; subcut to (40) 1" x 2" rectangles.

Solid yellow: Cut (3) 2 1/2" x 22" strips; subcut to (32) 2" x 2 1/2" rectangles.

White with yellow and green print: Cut (2) 2" x 22" strips; Subcut to (40) 1" x 2" rectangles.

Solid green: Cut (3) 2 1/2" x 22" strips; Subcut to (32) 2" x 2 1/2" rectangles.

White with green and yellow print: Cut (2) 2" x 22" strips; subcut to (40) 1" x 2" rectangles.

Solid light blue: Cut (3) 2 1/2" x 22" strips; subcut to (32) 2" x 2 1/2" rectangles.

White with red and light blue print: Cut (2) 2" x 22" strips; subcut to (40) 1" x 22" rectangles.

Templates B and C

Cut template B pieces from the same fabrics you used to make the arc units. Look at the photograph of Annie's quilt to see which template B piece is to be sewn to each arc unit.

Cut (2) 13 1/2" strips from the white with yellow print #1. Subcut to (4) 13 1/2" squares and set these aside for your appliqué block. From the remainder of the second 13 1/2" strip, cut as many of the 40 template C pieces as you can. If you need more, cut a 6" strip for the rest. Sew a template C piece to each arc. You will have (40) 3 1/2" arc units.

Refer to the photograph of Annie's quilt while arranging the arc units and 4-Patch units to make the five Dogwood Blossom blocks.

Appliqué Blocks

Use the pattern on page 30 for the appliquéd Dogwood Blossom adapted from *The Sister Blocks*, by Edie McGinnis. Use your favorite appliqué method and feel free to rearrange the pattern to fill the block as you wish.

When you have completed the appliqué, press the blocks, right side down, on a fluffy terry towel. Trim the blocks to 12 1/2" square.

Arrange the 5 pieced blocks and 4 appliqué blocks in 3 rows of 3 blocks each. You may wish to refer to Annie's quilt for placement.

BORDERS

Middle Border

Construct the middle border first as it will determine the width of the first border.

The middle border is made from a variety of 4-Patch units on point. Begin by pairing an assortment of prints with solid colors. For each 4-Patch unit, cut (2) 2" squares from a solid print and (2) 2" squares from a coordinating print. Make a total of (40) 4-Patch units, 8 from each of the 5 solid colors.

Cut (3) 5" strips from the white with yellow print #1; subcut to (18) 5" squares. Cut each square in half diagonally in both directions. You will have (72) 1/4-square triangles.

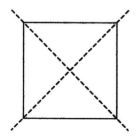

Cut (1) 2 3/4" strip from the white with yellow print #1; subcut to (8) 2 3/4" squares. Cut each square in half diagonally once. You will have (16) 1/2-square triangles.

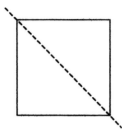

The middle border is constructed by sewing the 4-Patch units on point with 1/4-square setting triangles to finish. The ends of the strips are finished with the 1/2-square triangles. The strips will be sewn and then attached to the center of the quilt top as a long horizontal border: Measure through the vertical center of the quilt top and trim 2 strips to that measurement. Sew the strips to the sides of the quilt top. Press the seam allowanced toward the border strips.

Measure through the horizontal middle of the quilt top and trim 2 strips to that length. Sew the strips to the top and bottom of the quilt top. Press the seam allowances toward the borders strips.

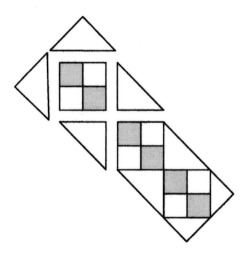

The shorter side strips have (9) 4-Patch units; the longer top and bottom strips have (11) 4-Patch units. Once you have sewn the elements of the strip, you will see that the setting triangles are oversized just a bit. This lets you trim the edges even and have a consistent 1/4" seam allowance.

Inner Border

Using strips cut from the length of the white with yellow print #1, make a long horizontal border, following the instructions above. Measure the length of the shorter strips for the inner border. The first border strip will have to be wide enough to enlarge the center to fit the middle border. Annie cut her inner border strips 1 1/4" wide, making the inner border just 3/4" inch wide when sewn. Press the seam allowances toward the inner border strips.

Outer Border

The outer border is a simple long horizontal border. Cut (4) 1/2" strips from the length of the white with yellow print #1 and follow the instructions above.

Annie rounded the corners of her quilt top before she added the piping and the binding. She may have used a saucer or bowl as a pattern to make the rounded corners consistent. You will find instructions for bias binding on page 122.

QUILTING

Annie machine quilted her work with yellow thread. In the pieced Dogwood blocks she created leaf designs, using the spikes as a guide for the edges of the palm-like leaves and adding veins. She echo quilted around the appliqué Dogwood Blossoms and quilted more flowers in the blank spaces. The 4-Patch border includes a leafy vine, and the outer border replicates the arcs and appliqué Dogwood Blossoms both.

Once you have completed the quilting and binding, don't forget to document and label your work!

A Garden Wall

85" x 85"
Made by Linda Carlson of Grand Lake, Colo.

Linda surrounded her Dogwood Blossom blocks with a
Brick Wall setting of rectangles. To enhance the wall effect,
Linda included an appliqué vine
with broderie perse flowers, dragonflies and butterflies.

Refer to the Dogwood Blossom pattern and templates on page 16. You will need to make templates for B and C. You will need 32 copies of the foundation for paper piecing. Piece A will be rotary cut and strip pieced following the instructions on page 113.

FABRIC REQUIREMENTS

1 1/4 yards yellow with white print (arc backgrounds, templates B and C pieces, 4-Patch units, bricks)

5/8 yard white with yellow print (spikes, 4-Patch units, bricks)

1 1/8 yards blue with white print (arc backgrounds, template C pieces, 4-Patch units, bricks)

7/8 yard white with blue print (spikes, template B pieces, 4-Patch units, bricks)

2 7/8 yards total assorted prints (bricks)

2 3/8 yards total assorted neutral prints (mortar)

1 1/4 yards green with white print (vines, leaves, binding)

1/4 yard yellow-green (leaves)

1 yard floral (broderie perse appliqué flowers)

Fat quarter of a print that has butterflies, dragonflies or birds (broderie perse appliqué)

1 1/4 yards white with green print (inner border)

2 1/2 yards floral print (outer border)

5 yards (backing)

CONSTRUCTING THE UNITS

4-Patch Units

Cut (2) 2" strips from the yellow with white print and (2) 2" strips from the white with yellow print. Sew the 2 strips together along the long edge and press the seam allowance toward the yellow print. Subcut the strip set into (24) 2" segments.

Cut (2) 2" strips from the blue with white print and (2) 2" strips from the white with blue print. Sew a blue print strip to each white print strip along the long edge and press the seam allowance toward the blue print. Subcut the strip sets into (32) 2" segments.

Sew 8 yellow segments to another 8 yellow segments, alternating the direction to create 8 yellow 4-Patch units. Sew 16 blue segments to another 16 blue segments, alternating the direction to create 16 blue 4-Patch units.

Cut (8) 2" squares from the white with blue print and (8) 2" squares from the yellow with white print. Sew a blue square to each yellow square and press the seam allowance toward the yellow. Sew the 4 blue and yellow segments to the 8 remaining yellow segments, alternating the direction so the yellow squares are opposite, to finish the 4-Patch units. You will have 8 yellow and blue 4-Patch units.

You should have a total of (32) 4-Patch units.

Arc Units

Refer to page 119 for instructions on Paper Foundation Piecing.

White with yellow print: Cut (2) 2" strips; subcut each strip into 1" x 2" rectangles. You need a total of 80 rectangles for the spikes.

Yellow with white print: Cut (4) 2 1/2" strips; subcut each strip into 2" x 2 1/2" rectangles. You need a total of (64) rectangles for the spike background.

Templates B and C

Cut 16 template B pieces and 16 template C pieces from the yellow with white print fabric. Cut 16 template B pieces from the white with blue print fabric. Cut 16 template C pieces from the blue with white print fabric.

Sew a yellow B piece and a yellow C piece to each yellow arc. Sew the blue B and C pieces to each blue arc. You will have (32) 3 1/2" arc units.

Refer to the quilt photograph while arranging the arc units and 4-Patch units into your block. When you sew the 4 blocks together, you will rotate them to create the "wreath" that appears in Linda's quilt.

INNER BORDER

Measure through the horizontal and vertical center of your quilt top. If all your seam allowances have been sewn with an accurate 1/4" seam, your top could measure 24 1/2" square.

From the white with green print, cut 4 strips from the length of the fabric. Remove the selvages and cut (8) 1/2" strips. Do not remove any length from the strips, even though they are longer than the sides of the center.

Find the center of each strip and match it to the center of each side. From the center mark of the border strip, measure out 12 1/2" (or half of what your top measures) and pin the strip to the top 1/4" from the end. Repeat in the other direction. When you sew the strip to the top, begin and end 1/4" from the end.

Refer to page 121 for instructions on how to make mitered corners.

THE BRICKS

Assorted prints (including those used in the Dogwood Blossom blocks): Cut 5 1/4" strips, then subcut the strips into 3" segments for a total of (306) 3" x 5 1/4" rectangles. You should be able to get 13 rectangles from each strip. Cut a total of (28) 3" x 2 7/8" rectangles from the assorted prints. These represent half-bricks but are not half the length of the brick rectangles. Be sure you do not just cut extra 3" x 5 1/4" rectangles and cut them in half.

Assorted neutral prints: Cut (44) 1" x 40" strips; subcut some of the strips into (214) 1" x 3" pieces.

Look at Linda's quilt. Notice that each row begins or ends with a 3" x 5 1/4" rectangle. Make 12 rows of bricks by sewing 13 whole bricks end to end, being sure to separate the bricks by a 1" x 3" neutral strip and to end with a partial brick. Press the seam allowances toward the neutral strips.

Sew 6 rows together into a segment by alternating the direction of the rows so that each one begins with a full brick or a partial brick. Separate each row of bricks with a strip of the neutral. Measure the length of the row of bricks. You will have to sew 2 neutral strips together, end to end, to have a strip long enough. The first and last rows of the segment will be a neutral strip. Press the seam allowances toward the neutral strips.

Make a second segment by sewing the 6 remaining rows together, again separating the strips with the neutral strip. The first and last rows of the segment will be a neutral strip. Set the 2 segments aside until you've made the side segments.

The rows on the sides each have either 3 whole bricks or 2 whole bricks and 2 partial bricks. Sew 14 rows of 3 whole bricks, separated by a 1" x 3" neutral strip. Sew 14 rows of 2 whole bricks that begin and end with partial bricks, also separated by 1" x 3" neutral strips. Press the seam allowance toward the neutral strips.

Sew 14 rows of bricks together. Begin with a row of 2 full bricks and 2 partial bricks and end with a row of 3 full bricks. Separate each row with a 1" x 15 3/4" neutral strip. (Measure your strips of bricks to make sure this is the correct length for the strip.) The segment begins and ends with a row of bricks. Press the seam allowances toward the neutral strips.

Sew together a second 14 rows of bricks. Begin with a row of 3 full bricks and end with a row of 2 full bricks and 2 partial bricks. Separate each row with a 1" x 15 3/4" neutral strip. Again, the segment begins and ends with a row of bricks. Press the seam allowances toward the neutral strips.

Measure through the vertical center of the Dogwood Blossom blocks and first border. If your seam allowances have been a consistent 1/4" it could measure 33". Cut (2) 1" x 33" strips and sew them to the sides of the quilt-top center. Press the seams toward the strips. Sew the side brick segments to the sides of the quilt-top center. Press the seams toward the strips. Take another look at Linda's quilt for guidance on how to orient the segments so the bricks will match up with the top and bottom segments.

Now sew the top and bottom segments to the quilt center. Be sure the side neutral strips match the small segments in the corners. The "wall" should look seamless. Press the seam allowances toward the neutral strips.

Measure through the vertical center of your quilt top. You will have to piece (2) 1" strips to get this length. Sew to the sides of the quilt top with a 1/4" seam allowance and press the seams toward the strips. Measure through the horizontal center of your quilt top. Sew (2) 1" strips to get this length. Sew the strips to the top and bottom of the quilt top. Press the seam allowances toward the strips.

OUTER BORDER

Floral print: Remove the selvages and cut (4) 6 1/2" strips the length of the fabric.

Measure through the center of your quilt top in both directions. If your seam allowances have been accurate, your quilt top could measure 72" in both directions. Find the center of the border strips and match it to the center of each side of your quilt top. Find the center of each strip and match it to the center of each side. From the center mark of the border strip, measure out 36" (or half of what your top measures) and pin the strip to the top 1/4" from the end. Repeat in the other direction. When you sew the strip to the top, begin and end 1/4" from the end.

Refer to page 121 for instructions on how to make mitered corners.

APPLIQUÉD VINES

Linda created a diagonal design of appliquéd vines. She used the green with white print fabric to sew bias tubes and make lots of appliquéd leaves. She used a second shade for some of the greens.

Linda surrounded the center Dogwood Blossom blocks with the vines and then let the vines "grow" across the wall. I have included a template for the leaves on her quilt. You will want to study the photograph to see how you might arrange a 1/2" bias vine or use your own design sense. I encourage you to arrange the vines and leaves as you please.

Linda cut the flowers from the floral fabric and scattered them across her vine. She fused the raw-edged flowers to the quilt top. You may use the appliqué method you favor.

She cut the butterflies and/or dragonflies from a print that included both (you may use butterflies, dragonflies or birds or any combination of them) and attached them to the quilt top. Some of the butterflies are appliquéd with the sewing machine and have raw edges, but some are double-sided. That is, she cut 2 identical butterflies and fused them, wrong sides together. She then attached the butterflies to the quilt top through the body so the wings are free, adding a dimensional touch. Follow the same procedure for dragonflies or birds.

QUILTING

Linda quilted "in the ditch" on either side of each neutral strip and on either side of the stems and around each of the leaves. She worked veins in the leaves and also stitched just inside the raw edges of the flowers, quilting and permanently securing the flowers at the same time. She then quilted a cross-hatch design in each brick; a meandering design finishes the outside border.

BINDING

From the green with white print, cut (9) 2 1/2" strips. Refer to page 122 for instructions on making a straight-edge binding.

Template for leaf

Add 1/4" seam allowance to fabric

Aunt Niece's Cedar Tree

54" x 54"
Made by Tara Didier and Melissa Ulmen of Eltopia, Wash.

"Aunt Niece" refers to the fact that Tara is Melissa's aunt, and they made the quilt together. The 36 blocks in this quilt only look complicated. By changing the values and fabrics in the Little Cedar Tree block, Tara and Melissa created a very interesting design.

FABRIC REQUIREMENTS

1/3 yard red solid (blocks)
3/4 yard white solid (blocks)
3/4 yard white with blue print (blocks)
1 1/2 yards blue with white and red print (blocks and
    border)
1/3 yard blue with white print (blocks)
1/4 yard red with white print (blocks)
7/8 yard blue solid (blocks, binding)
1/2 yard white with red print (blocks)
1/4 yard red with white print #1 (blocks)
1/3 yard white with red and blue (blocks)
1/4 yard red with white and blue (blocks)
3 1/4 yards backing

CUTTING INSTRUCTIONS

Unless otherwise noted, all strips are cut 4 7/8" wide. Practically every part of every block is a 1/2-square triangle unit that measures 4" finished.

Red solid: Cut (2) strips; subcut (11) 4 7/8" squares and
    (4) 4 1/2" squares.
White solid: Cut (5) strips; subcut (36) 4 7/8" squares.
White with blue print: Cut (4) strips; subcut
    (28) 4 7/8" squares.
Blue with white and red print: Cut (4) 56" strips from the
    length of the fabric and cut (4) 4 7/8" squares.
Blue with white print: Cut (2) 4 7/8" squares.
Red with white print: Cut (1) strip; subcut (4) 4 7/8"
    squares.
Blue solid: Cut (2) strips; subcut (10) 4 7/8" squares and
    (4) 4 1/2" squares.
White with red print: Cut (2) 8 1/2" strips; subcut (8) 8
    1/2" squares.
Red with white and blue print #1: Cut (1) strip; subcut (6)
    4 7/8" squares.
White with red and blue print: Cut (2) strips; subcut (12)
    4 7/8" squares.
Red with white and blue print #2: Cut (1) strip; subcut (4)
    4 7/8" squares.

CONSTRUCTING THE BLOCKS

Of the 36 blocks in Tara and Melissa's quilt, 28 are made of (4) 1/2-square triangle units in varying fabric pairs. Refer to page 29 for instructions for making the 1/2-square triangle units. Refer to the graphic of each block for placement of the 1/2-square triangle units in the 4-Patch. Not all 28 blocks are Little Cedar Tree blocks but they are all 4-Patch blocks.

Block #1

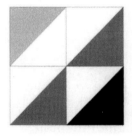

For 4 blocks, pair 4 solid white squares and 4 red with white and blue print #1 squares. Pair 2 white solid squares with 2 white with red print squares. Pair 2 solid white squares with 2 solid red squares.

Block #2

You will make 4 blocks with the (4) 8 1/2" white with red prints squares and (4) 4 1/2" blue solid squares; and 4 blocks with the remaining (4) 8 1/2" white with red print squares and (4) 4 1/2" red solid squares.

Place a blue solid square in the lower right corner of the white with red print square, right sides together. Draw a line diagonally from the upper right corner to the lower left corner on the wrong side of the blue square. Sew on the line with your sewing machine. Fold the square over the stitching, matching the corner. Press and remove the center layer of fabric. Repeat with the red solid squares and the remaining 8 1/2" white with red print squares. You will have 8 blocks.

Block #3

For 4 blocks, pair 2 white solid squares with 2 blue solid squares. Pair 2 white solid squares with 2 white with blue print squares. Pair 4 white with red print squares with 4 blue solid squares.

Block #4

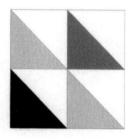

For 4 blocks, pair 4 white solid squares with 4 white with red and blue print squares. Pair 2 white solid squares with 2 red with white and blue print #1 squares. Pair 2 white with solid squares with 2 blue solid squares.

Block #5

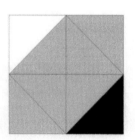

The coloring in this block is a bit different. Two 1/2-square triangle units are made from just one fabric, so you may choose to make 4 1/2" squares from the white with blue print instead of a 1/2-square triangle unit. Removing the seam may alter the continuity of the blocks and the overall look of the quilt.

For 8 blocks, pair 4 white solid squares with 4 white with blue print squares. Pair 4 blue with white and red print squares with 4 white with blue print squares. Pair 16 white with blue print squares for a total of (16) 1/2-square triangle units. (Or cut (16) 4 1/2" squares.)

Block #6

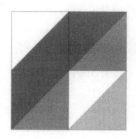

For 4 blocks, pair 2 white solid squares with 2 red solid squares. Pair 2 white solid white squares with 2 white with blue print squares. Pair 4 red solid red squares with 4 white with red and blue print squares.

Block #7

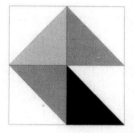

For a total of 4 blocks, pair 2 white solid squares with 2 red with white print squares. Pair 4 white solid squares with 4 red with white and blue #2 print squares. Pair 2 white solid squares with to blue with white print squares.

CONSTRUCTING THE QUILT TOP

Refer to the photograph of Tara and Melissa's quilt for placement of the blocks. Notice that rows 1 and 6, rows 2 and 5, and rows 3 and 4 are identical, just flipped.

BORDER

Cut each border strip in half so it measures 4 1/2" by about 28." Place a solid red square on one end of 4 of the strips, right sides together. Draw a diagonal line on the squares as is shown in the graphic below.

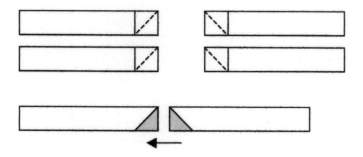

Place a solid blue square on the remaining 4 strips, right sides together. Draw a diagonal line on the squares as you did on the red. Sew on the lines. Fold the square over the stitching, matching the corner. Press and remove the center layer of fabric.

Sew 2 strips together, matching the triangle ends. Repeat for a total of 4 border strips.

Match the triangles to the correct sides of the quilt top. Refer to page 121 for instructions on a mitered border.

QUILTING

Tara and Melissa machine quilted an overall meandering design.

BINDING

This binding is unique. The binding strips were wrapped around the edge and sewn with the machine. On the front and the back of the quilt, the binding is raw-edged. Washing the quilt has raveled the raw edge and given the binding a ruffled look. Tara and Melissa say it gives the quilt an "old-time look."

Don't forget to finish your quilt by documenting its name, your name, where you live and when you made it.

Dream Weaver

65" x 66 3/4"
Made by Rita J. Feely, Independence, Mo.

Rita was drawn to the Spider Web block because of her love of crazy quilts.

"Dream Weaver" reminds her of the hopes and dreams and

the paths each of our lives take.

The intertwined feather quilting represents the way our lives touch each other.

FABRIC REQUIREMENTS

1 1/3 yards red solid (center Spider Web blocks, triangle units, borders)

3 yards navy solid (center Spider Web blocks, triangle units, borders, binding)

1 1/3 yards white with navy print (center Spider Web blocks, border)

2 yards white with navy and red print (center Spider Web blocks, border)

3 yards navy with white and red print (center Spider Web blocks, triangle units, border)

3/4 yard red with white and navy print (center Spider Web blocks, border)

1 1/2 yards yellow with white print (corner triangle units)

1/2 yard red with white print (corner triangles, border)

4 yards backing fabric

CENTER SPIDER WEB BLOCKS
CUTTING INSTRUCTIONS

Using the individual templates on page 14 to make this quilt will take less fabric. The amount of fabric figured is based on strip piecing and using the specialty ruler and rotary cutting. There will be fabric left over.

Red solid: Cut (7) 2 1/2" strips.

Navy solid: Cut (7) 4 7/8" strips. Cut (3) 4 3/8" strips; subcut (14) 4 3/8" squares. Cut each square in half diagonally for (28) 1/2-square triangles.

White with navy print: Cut (7) 4 7/8" strips.

White with red and navy print: Cut (3) 2 1/2" strips.

Navy with white and red print: Cut (2) 2 1/2" strips. Cut (1) 4 3/8" strip; subcut (4) 4 3/8" squares. Cut each square in half diagonally for (8) 1/2-square triangles.

Red with white and navy print: Cut (2) 2 1/2" strips.

Strips sets

Sew (5) 2 1/2" red solid strips to (5) 4 7/8" white with navy print strips. Using the specialty ruler, cut 28 wedges.

Sew (2) 2 1/2" red strips to (2) 4 7/8" navy strips. Cut 12 wedges

Sew (1) 2 1/2" white with red and navy print strip to (1) 4 7/8" white with navy print strip. Cut 4 wedges.

Sew (2) 2 1/2" white with red and navy print strips to (2) 4 7/8" navy strips. Cut 12 wedges.

Sew (2) 2 1/2" navy with white and red strips to (2) 4 7/8" navy strips. Cut 8 wedges.

Sew (1) 2 1/2" red with white and navy print strip to (1) 4 7/8" white with navy print strip. Cut 4 wedges.

Sew (1) 2 1/2" red with white and navy print strip to (1) 4 7/8" navy strip. Cut 4 wedges.

Arrange the wedges and 1/2-square triangles into blocks according to the diagrams below. You will make 9 blocks, 1 Block A and 4 each of Block B and Block C.

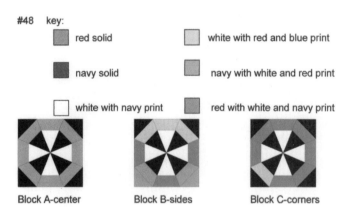

Block A-center   Block B-sides   Block C-corners

Block A: Center (make 1): 4 navy solid/red with white and navy print wedges, 4 white with navy print/red solid with white and navy print wedges, 4 navy solid 1/2-square triangles.

Block B: Sides (make 4): 2 white with red and navy print/navy wedges, 1 white with red print and navy solid/white with navy print wedge, 3 red solid/white with navy print wedge, 2 navy with white and red print/navy solid wedges, 2 navy solid 1/2-square triangles, 2 navy with white and red print 1/2-square triangles.

Block C: Corners (make 4): 1 white with red and navy print/white with navy print wedge, 3 red solid/navy solid wedges, 4 red solid/white with navy print wedges, 4 navy solid 1/2-square triangles.

Refer to the photograph of Rita's quilt for placement of the blocks. Notice that they rotate around the center. Sew the 9 blocks together, 3 rows of 3 blocks each.

Cut (2) 2 1/2" red solid strips and (2) 2 1/2" navy solid strips. Measure through the vertical and horizontal centers of the quilt top. If you have sewn with an accurate 1/4" seam allowance, your top will measure about 36 1/2" square.

Trim the red and navy strips to the quilt top's measurement. Sew a red solid strip to one side of the quilt top, stopping about 3 inches from the end. Sew a navy strip to the side to the left of the red strip, sewing all the way to the end. To the third side, to the left, sew a navy strip. Your last strip will be red. When the fourth strip is added, go back and complete strip #1.

CORNER TRIANGLE UNIT CUTTING INSTRUCTIONS

Navy with white and red: Cut (2) 4" strips; subcut (14) 4" squares. Cut each square in half diagonally for (28) 1/2-square triangles. Cut (10) 4 5/8" strips.

White with navy and red print: Cut (5) 2 3/8" strips.

Yellow with white print: Cut (2) 6" strips; subcut 12 wedges with the specialty ruler.

Cut (1) 4" strip; Subcut (6) 4" squares. Cut each square in half diagonally for (12) 1/2-square triangles.

Red with white print: Cut (5) 2 3/8" strips.

Strip sets

Sew (5) 2 3/8" strips from white with navy and red print to (5) 5 4/8" strips from navy with white and red print. Cut 30 wedges with the specialty ruler.

Sew (5) 2 3/8" strips from red with white to (5) 4 5/8" strips from navy with white and red print. Cut 30 wedges.

Arrange the wedges and 1/2-square triangles into blocks according to the diagrams below; 2 are partial blocks and 2 are whole blocks.

Block #1 and #3

Block #2 and #4

Block #1: Partial block (make 4): 3 red with white/navy with white and red wedges, 1 yellow with white print wedge, 1 yellow with white print 1/2-square triangle, 2 navy with white and red 1/2-square triangles. Trim the blocks across the diagonal, adding 1/4-inch seam allowance.

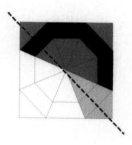

Block #2: Whole block (make 2): 7 red with white/navy with white and red wedges, 1 yellow with white print wedge, 1 yellow with white print 1/2-square triangle, 3 navy with white and red 1/2-square triangles.

Block #3: Partial block (make 4): 3 white with navy and red print/navy with white and red print wedges, 1 yellow with white print wedge, 1 yellow with white print 1/2-square triangle, 2 navy with white and red print 1/2-square triangles.

Block #4: Whole block (make 2): 7 white with navy and red print/navy with white and red print wedges, 1 yellow with white print wedge, 1 yellow with white print 1/2-square triangle, 3 navy with white and red print 1/2-square triangles.

Refer to the photograph of Rita's quilt to see which blocks and partial blocks form the 4 triangles and sew them together.

Cut (4) 2 1/4" red solid strips and (4) 2 1/4" navy solid strips. Cut (8) 1 1/2" yellow with white strips. These strips will frame the triangle units on the short sides. Sew a yellow strip to each of the red and navy strips, pressing the seam allowances toward the darker fabric. Sew these strips to the short side of the 4 triangle units, stopping 1/4" from the 90-degree angle. Refer to page XX for instructions on mitering the corners.

Sew the triangle units to the sides of the quilt top, setting the center square on point. Refer to the photograph of Rita's quilt for placement of the triangle units.

OUTSIDE BORDER CUTTING INSTRUCTIONS

Navy with white and red print: Cut (1) 4 3/8" strips; subcut (10) 4 3/8" squares. Cut each square in half diagonally for (20) 1/2-square triangles. Cut (4) 3 3/4" strips; subcut (8) 3 3/4" x 20" strips.

Red solid: Cut (3) 4 3/8" strips.

Red with white and navy print: Cut (5) 2 1/4" strips.

White with navy and red print: Cut (4) 2 /14" strips.

Navy solid: Cut (2) 4 3/8" strips.

White with navy print: Cut (2) 4 3/8" strips. Cut (4) 2 3/4" strip; Subcut (8) 2 3/4" x 20" strips.

Strip sets

Sew 3 red with white and navy print strips to 3 red solid strips. Cut 16 wedges with the specialty ruler.

Sew 2 red with white and navy print strips to two navy with red and white print strips. Cut 12 wedges.

Sew 2 white with navy and red print strips to 2 navy solid strips. Cut 12 wedges.

Sew 2 white with navy and red print strips to 2 white and navy print strips. Cut 8 wedges.

Arrange the wedges and 1/2-square triangles into blocks according to the diagrams below. Each is a partial block, 4 being half-blocks and 4 three-quarter blocks.

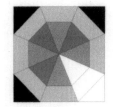

Block B1   **Block B2**

Block B1: Half block (make 4): 3 white with navy and red print/navy solid wedges, 2 white with navy and red print/white with navy print wedges, 2 navy solid 1/2-square triangles. Trim the blocks across the center, adding 1/4-inch seam allowance.

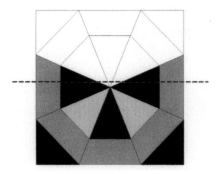

Block B2: 3/4 block (make 4): 4 red with white and navy print/red solid wedges, 3 red with white and navy print/navy with white and red print wedges, 3 navy solid 1/2-square triangles.

As you sew the wedges together, stop 1/4" from the point of the wedge. This will allow you to sew the rest of the border into the corner blocks, pivoting at the corner. Trim the side and bottom wedge in half, adding 1/4" seam allowance. The corner of the quilt top is the final 1/4 of the block.

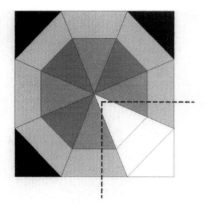

Sew a 2 3/4" x 20" white with navy print strip to each of the 3 3/4" x 20" strips. Press the seam allowance toward the darker fabric. Sew a strip set to either side of the 4 Block B1s. Refer to the photograph of Rita's quilt for placement.

Measure your quilt top. You may have to trim the strip set to about 16 3/4". You will have to determine the length based on your quilt top. Remember to account for the corner blocks, about 5 1/2".

Sew the borders onto the quilt top, pivoting at the corners, taking care to match the center of the Spider Web block with the mitered corner of the triangle units.

QUILTING

Rita machine quilted feathered wreaths and free-motion feathers over the entire surface.

BINDING

Refer to page 122 for instructions on straight binding.

XO

47" x 47"
Made by Judy Hitchcock of Rice, Minn.

Judy suggests that this pattern is for the experienced quilter "as it has 868 individual pieces." Judy paper foundation pieced the arcs and hand quilted her entry to reflect the era suggested by the fabric. She says, "Designing and constructing this quilt was fun, but definitely had me thinking 'outside the box!'"

Refer to the Dogwood Blossom pattern and templates on page 16. You will need to make templates for B and C. You will need 68 copies of the foundation for paper piecing. Piece A will be rotary cut and strip pieced following the instructions on page 113.

FABRIC REQUIREMENTS

5/8 yard red (spikes)
1 1/8 yards blue/red print (spike background)
1 3/4 yards cream (background for arcs, 4-Patch units, Inner Border #1)
1/4 yard green/blue/orange print (4-Patch units)
1/4 yard blue (inner border #2)
1/4 yard yellow (inner border #3)
2 2/3 yards green print (outer border, binding, backing. You'll use the 9" strip leftover from the border and binding to piece the backing.)

CONSTRUCTING THE UNITS

4-Patch Units
Cream fabric: Cut (3) 2" strips.
Green/blue/orange print: Cut (3) 2" strips.

Sew a cream strip to each print strip along the long edge and press the seam allowance toward the print.
Pairing (2) 2" units, invert 1 and sew them together, creating the 4-Patch block units. You will need (24) 4-Patch block units to complete the quilt. These units should measure 3 1/2" square.

Arc Units
Refer to page 119 for instructions on Paper Foundation Piecing.

Red fabric: Cut (9) 2" strips; subcut each strip into 1" x 2" rectangles. You need 340 rectangles for the spikes.
Blue/red print: Cut (14) 2 1/2" strips; subcut each strip into 2" x 2 1/2" rectangles.

You need 272 rectangles for the spike background.

Templates B and C
Cut out 68 template B pieces and 68 template C pieces from the cream fabric. Sew a B piece and a C piece to each arc. You will have (68) 3 1/2" arc units.
Cream fabric: Cut (1) 3 1/2" strip; subcut the strip into (8) 3 1/2" squares.

Refer to the photograph of Judy's quilt while arranging the arc units, 4-Patch units and 3 1/2" squares. There are 10 units in each of 10 rows. Sew the units into rows and then sew the rows together to ready the quilt top for borders. Measure through the center of the quilt top. At this point, if you have sewn your 1/4" seams accurately, your top may measure 30 1/2" square.

BORDERS

Inner Border #1: Cut (4) 2" strips from the cream.
Inner Border #2: Cut (4) 1 1/4" strips from the blue.
Inner Border #3: Cut (4) 1 5/8" strips from the yellow.
Outer Border: Cut (4) 5 1/4" strips from the length of the green print fabric. Remove the selvages and cut the strips parallel to the selvage edge.

Measure through the vertical center of the quilt top. Cut (2) 2" cream strips the same length as the vertical measurement. Sew the strips to the sides. Press the seam allowance toward the strips.
Measure through the horizontal center of the quilt top. Cut the 2 remaining 2" cream strips the same length as the horizontal measurement. Sew the strips to the top and bottom. Press the seam allowance toward the strips.
Measure through the vertical center of the quilt top again. Cut 2 blue strips that length. Sew the strips to the sides. Press the seam allowance toward the strips.
Measure through the horizontal center of the quilt top again. Cut the 2 remaining blue strips the same length. Sew the strips to the top and bottom. Press the seam allowance toward the strips.
Measure through the vertical center of the quilt top a third time. Cut 2 yellow strips that length. Sew the strips to the sides. Press the seam allowance toward the strips.
Measure through the horizontal center of the quilt top a third time. Cut the remaining 2 yellow strips that length. Sew the strips to the top and bottom and press the seam allowance toward the strips.
Once again, measure through the vertical center of the quilt top. Cut (2) 5 1/2" green print strips that length. Sew the strips to the sides of the quilt top and press the seam allowances toward the strips.
Measure through the horizontal center of the quilt top. Cut the remaining (2) 5 1/2" green print strips that as the horizontal measurement. Sew the strips to the top and bottom and press the seam allowances toward the strips.

QUILTING

Judy hand quilted her project. She worked a single line diagonally through the top from corner to corner, inside the borders, and quilted 1/4" outside each arc. She quilted in the ditch just inside the second and the fourth border. The outer border is quilted in a braid design with rows 1 1/2" apart.

BINDING

Cut (4) 2 1/2" strips from the length of the remaining green print fabric for binding a straight border. Refer to page 122 for directions.

The remaining piece of green print will be sewn to the backing fabric to make a piece large enough to back the finished quilt top.

Springtime in the Cedars

44" x 52 3/4"
Made by Maxine Kline of Daphne, Ala.

Study Maxine's quilt and you'll find that she created a variety of blocks using the Little Cedar Tree as an element.

By changing the size and coloration of the Little Cedar Tree block, she created at least 15 distinctly different blocks!

Isn't a springtime forest of cedars filled with such variations?

FABRIC REQUIREMENTS

11 fat quarters yellow, white and green prints with splashes of red (blocks)
1 fat quarter green solid (blocks)
1 fat quarter yellow solid (blocks)
1/2 yard red solid #1 (blocks, binding)
1/2 yard red solid #2 (border)
2 yards yellow with white print (background and setting triangles)
2 yards backing (you will need to piece the back to make it large enough)

CUTTING INSTRUCTIONS

Refer to page 111 for instructions to make the Little Cedar Tree block.

6-inch finished block: Make 11

Yellow, white and green prints: For 10 blocks, cut (2) 3 7/8" squares from each fabric.
Green solid: For 1 block cut (2) 3 7/8" squares.
Yellow and white background print: Cut (3) 3 7/8" strips; subcut (22) 3 7/8" squares.

3-inch finished block: Make 15

Yellow, white and green prints: For 13 blocks, cut (2) 2 3/8" squares from each fabric.
Green solid: For 1 block, cut (2) 2 3/8" squares.
Yellow solid: For 1 block cut (2) 2 3/8" squares.
Yellow and white background print: Cut (2) 2 3/8" strips; subcut (30) 2 3/8" squares.
Cut (4) 6 1/2" strips; subcut (17) 3 1/2" x 6 1/2" rectangles and (10) 6 1/2" squares. Cut (3) 3 1/2" strips; subcut (28) 3 1/2" squares.

1 1/2-inch finished block: Make 9

Yellow, white and green prints: For 8 blocks, cut (2) 1 5/8" squares from each of several fabrics.
Yellow solid: For 1 block, cut (2) 1 5/8" squares. Cut (1) 2" square.
Yellow and white background print: Cut (1) 1 5/8" strip; Subcut (18) 1 5/8" squares. Cut (3) 2" squares.
Green solid: Cut (2) 2" squares.
Red solid #1: Cut (1) 2" square and (4) 3 1/2" squares.

Use your creativity to make the blocks. The illustrations on page 58 will give you an idea of how Maxine arranged some of her fabrics and Little Cedar Tree blocks. The important thing is that you sprinkle the very dramatic elements over the quilt top.

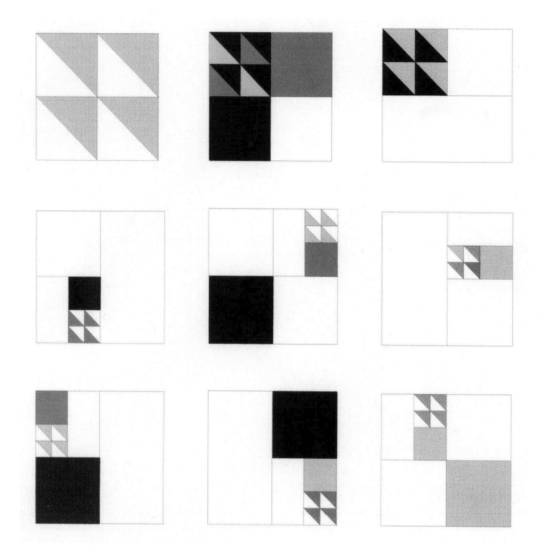

CONSTRUCTING THE QUILT TOP

Yellow and white background print: Cut (1) 9 1/4" strip; subcut (4) 9 1/4" squares. Cut each square in half diagonally in both directions for (18) 1/4-square triangles needed for the side setting triangles. Cut (2) 7" squares. Cut both squares in half diagonally for (4) 1/2-square triangles needed for the corner triangles.

Refer to page 63 for instructions on how to construct the on-point setting. This quilt is done the same way but with no sashing.

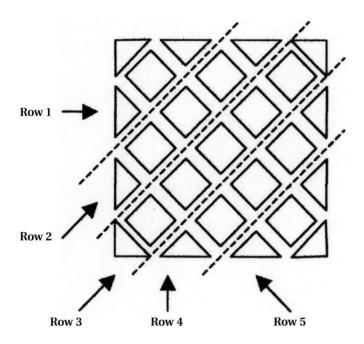

BORDER

Red solid #2: Cut (6) 2" strips. If your fabric is not 44" wide, you may have to cut another strip and cut it into (2) 2" strips.

Measure through the vertical center of the quilt top. Sew 4 strips together, end to end, for 2 strips. Trim the 2 strips to the length of your quilt top and sew them to the sides. Press the seam allowance toward the strip.

Measure through the horizontal center of your quilt top. Piece full strips and half strips if the full strips aren't long enough. Trim to the horizontal measurement and sew the strips to the top and bottom. Press the seam allowance toward the strip.

QUILTING

Maxine machine quilted an all-over design that was at one time called Elbow Quilting because one used one's elbow as the pivot point when drawing concentric arcs. The design is also called Baptist Fan.

BINDING

Maxine used red solid #1 to finish her quilt. Refer to page 122 for instructions on finishing with a straight-edge binding.

Maxine documented her quilt with a preprinted label, available on the bolt at your local quilt shop.

Honoring Those Kansas City Designing Women

37 1/2"x 37 1/2"
Made by Linda Birch Mooney of Shawnee, Kan.

Linda combined the Maple Leaf block with the Little Cedar Tree block and added appliqué designs from Barbara Brackman's book "Women of Design" (Kansas City Star Books; 2004).

FABRIC REQUIREMENTS

1 7/8 yards blue with white print (Maple Leaf blocks, Little Cedar block, appliqué, second border, binding)

3/4 yard yellow with white and blue print (Maple Leaf blocks, Little Cedar block)

5/8 yard solid blue (sashing, first border, appliqué)

1/4 yard white with blue and red print (corner stones, appliqué)

7/8 yard yellow with white print (appliqué blocks, setting triangles)

1/8 yard yellow with pink and red floral print (appliqué)

Assorted white, yellow and green prints equaling about 1/4 yard (appliqué)

1 1/8 yard for backing

CUTTING INSTRUCTIONS

Blue with white print: Cut (2) 1 3/8" strips; subcut (48) 1 3/8" squares. Cut (2) 1 3/4" strips; subcut (32) 1 3/4" squares. Cut (5) 4" strips: subcut (2) 4" squares from 1 strip and set aside the remaining 4 strips for Border #2.

Yellow with white and blue print: Cut (2) 1 3/8" strips; subcut (48) 1 3/8" squares. Cut (2) 1 3/4" strips; subcut (32) 1 3/4" squares. Cut (1) 3 3/8" strip; subcut (16) 1 3/8" x 3 3/8" rectangles. Cut (1) 4" square; subcut (2) 4" squares.

Solid blue: Cut (2) 6 1/2" strips; Subcut (36) 1 1/2" x 6 1/2" rectangles. Cut (4) 1 1/2" strips and set aside for Border #1.

White with blue and red print: Cut (1) 1 1/2" strip; subcut (24) 1 1/2" squares.

Yellow with white print: Cut (2) 7 1/2" strips; subcut (8) 7 1/2" squares. Cut (1) 9 3/4" strip; subcut (2) 9 3/4" squares and cut each square in half diagonally in both directions for (8) 1/4-square triangles. Cut (2) 5 1/2" squares; cut in half diagonally once for (8) 1/2-square triangles.

MAPLE LEAF BLOCKS

Pair a 1 3/4" blue with white print square with a 1 3/4" yellow with white and blue print square, right sides together. Draw a line diagonally across the wrong side of the lighter square and sew 1/4" from the line on both sides of the line. Cut on the line and press the (2) 1/2-square units open, pressing the seam allowance toward the blue and white print. Repeat for (64) 1/2-square triangle units. Trim each 1/2-square unit to measure 1 3/8" square.

Make (16) 3 1/4" bias tape pieces to appliqué to 16 1 3/8" yellow with white and blue print squares.

Refer to the instructions on page 112 for constructing the Maple Leaf Block. Make four Maple Leaf blocks.

LITTLE CEDAR TREE BLOCK

Make (4) 1/2-square triangle units by pairing each of the 4" blue with white print squares with a 4" yellow with white and blue squares. Trim the (4) 1/2-square triangle units to 3 1/2" square. Sew the (4) 3 1/2" 1/2-square triangle units into a 4-Patch block. Refer to Linda's quilt for placement of the units.

Appliqué Carlie's Wild Rose design in the center.

APPLIQUÉ BLOCKS

Using your favorite appliqué method and the assortment of white, yellow and green prints, appliqué Katie's Wild Rose on (4) 7 1/2" yellow with white print blocks. Appliqué Eveline's Posey on the remaining (4) 7 1/2" yellow with white print blocks. When the appliqués are complete, press, right-side down, on a fluffy terrycloth towel and trim the blocks to 6 1/2" square.

SASHING

Sew a sashing piece to the right of each block, pressing the seam allowance toward the sashing piece.

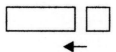

Sew a 1 1/2" blue with white and red print square to the end of (19) sashing pieces and press the seam allowance toward the sashing piece. Sew (13) of these units to the top of each of the blocks. The blocks now have a sashing piece on the top and right sides.

Arrange your blocks, referring to the photograph of Linda's quilt for placement. Sew 5 of the remaining sashing units to the left side of the blocks that are on the left and bottom of the arrangement. Sew the remaining 4 to

Carlie's Wild Rose

Eveline's Posey

Katie's Wild Rose

Flowers and Leaves for corners

Add 1/4" seam allowance to fabric

the bottom of the blocks on the right side and the bottom (not the one in the bottom right corner).

You should have 1 sashing piece and (2) 1 1/2" squares left. Sew the squares to each end of the rectangle and press the seam allowance toward the sashing piece. Sew this unit to the bottom of the block in the lower right corner of your arrangement.

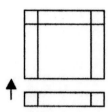

Sew the blocks together in rows, adding the setting triangles as the diagram shows. The first row will have both a 1/2-square triangle and (2) 1/4-square triangles. Each row after will begin and end with a 1/4-square until you reach the corners. Once you have arranged your blocks and added the sashing pieces, you can fill in with the triangles.

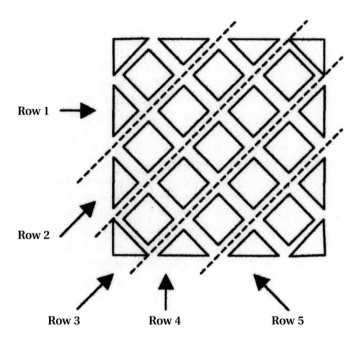

Row 1 →

Row 2

Row 3   Row 4   Row 5

FINISHING THE CENTER

You will notice that the setting triangles you cut are oversized. This will allow you to trim the edges after the center of the top is constructed and before the border is added. In trimming, you will be removing the outside half of the 1 1/2" cornerstone blocks that appear around the outside edge as well as straightening the edges, leaving 1/4" seam allowance. (Please note: The diagram below shows only a small portion of the top for illustration purposes.)

Trim the edges, leaving 1/4" seam allowance

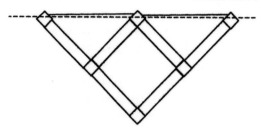

BORDER #1

Measure through the vertical center of your quilt top. Trim (2) 1 1/2" solid blue strips to that measurement and sew to the sides of the quilt top. Measure through the horizontal center of the quilt top; trim the remaining (2) 1 1/2" solid blue strips to that measurement and sew to the top and bottom of your quilt top.

BORDER #2

Remeasure your quilt top and trim the (4) 4" strips to that measurement plus 8" each. Find the center of the strips and match them to the center of the edge of the quilt top. Sew each strip to the quilt, starting and stopping 1/4" from the corner of the quilt top.

Refer to page 12 for mitering the corner of the border.

Appliqué flowers and leaves in the corners.

QUILTING

Linda hand quilted her design with a variety of colored threads. She used the same designs for quilting the side setting triangles as she did to appliqué the blocks. She quilted a vine of leaves between the appliqué in the corners.

BINDING

Refer to page 125 for directions for making a scalloped border and bias binding.

Documenting your quilt is important. Linda made a pocket on the back of her quilt that is just the right size for the booklet "Patterns of History 1930-1950: Pick a Pack – Pick a Pattern." Keeping the booklet with the quilt will let Linda's descendants completely understand what inspired its creation.

Murphy's Law

36" x 36"
Made by Jane Morse of Lynnwood, Was

Jane said she was adapting weaving designs for a series of quilts when she learned of the Patterns of History Challenge. Noting that the Comfort Quilt block was perfect for the circular design she was working with, she combined the two projects and came up with this wonderful quilt. It has been quite a challenge for me to figure out how she did it. Finally seeing the individual blocks was an "ah-ha!" moment.

FABRIC REQUIREMENTS

1 yard green with white print
1/4 yard white with blue and red print
5/8 yard white with green and yellow print #1
5/8 yard white with green and yellow print #2
1/8 yard red with white print
3/8 yard yellow with white and green print
1 1/4 yards for backing

BLOCKS CUTTING AND CONSTRUCTION

Block #1:
6 1/2" x 6 1/2" finished (make 1)

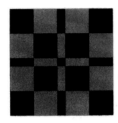

Green and white print: Cut (1) 2" strip; subcut (1) 2" x 17" strip and (4) 2" x 1" rectangles.
White with red and blue print: Cut (1) 2" strip; subcut (1) 2" x 17" strip, (4) 2" x 1" rectangles and (1) 1" square.

Refer to page 110 for instructions on making 4-Patch units.

Sew the 17" strips together and press the seam allowance toward the green print. Subcut the strip to (8) 2" segments and (4) 1" segments. Sew the (4) 4-Patch units. Sew 2 of the units to either side of (1) 1" segments, making sure the 1" unit is turned as in Jane's block.

Sew 2 of the 1" units to either side of the 1" square. Sew the 3 rows together, referring to the block for clarification.

Block #2:
6 1/2" x 4 1/2" finished (make 4)

Green with white print: Cut (2) 1 1/2" strips and set aside. Cut (1) 2" strip; subcut (8) 2" x 1" rectangles and (4) 1" squares.

White with green and yellow print #1: Cut (2) 1 1/2" strips and set aside. Cut (1) 2" strip; subcut (8) 2" x 1" rectangles.

Sew the 2 reserved strips together along a long edge and press the seam allowance toward the green strip. Cut the strip set into (32) 2" segments and (16) 1" segments. Follow the instructions for Block #1 to complete a total of 4 blocks.

Block #3:
4 1/2" x 4 1/2" finished (make 4)

Green with white print: Cut (2) 1 1/2" strips; subcut (16) 1 1/2" x 3" rectangles and (16) 1 1/2" x 1" rectangles.
White with green and yellow print #2: Cut (1) 1 1/2" strip; subcut (32) 1 1/2" squares and (4) 1" squares.

Refer to page 110 for instructions in making the Comfort Quilt block.

Block #4:
4 1/2" x 6" finished (make 8)

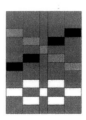

Green with white print: Cut (6) 1 1/2" strips; subcut (64) 1 1/2" squares, (32) 1 1/2" x 2" rectangles and (56) 1 1/2" x 1" rectangles. Cut (1) 2 1/2" strip; subcut (16) 2 1/2" x 1" rectangles.
Red with white print: Cut (1) 1 1/2" strip; subcut (32) 1 1/2" x 1" rectangles and (8) 1" squares.

White with blue and red print: Cut (1) 1 1/2" strip; subcut
(32) 1 1/2" x 1" rectangles.
Yellow with white and green print: Cut (2) 1 1/2" strips;
subcut (48) 1 1/2" x 1" rectangles and (4) 1" squares.

This block is constructed by sewing vertical rows.
Refer to the photograph of Jane's quilt for fabric placement. It is very important that you sew with an accurate
1/4" seam allowance.

Block #5:
6 1/2" x 6" finished (make 4)

Green with white print: Cut (1) 3" strip; subcut (4) 3" x 7"
rectangles. Cut (4) 1" strips; subcut (4) 1" x 7" rectangles, (16) 1" squares and (48) 1" x 2" rectangles.
White with blue and red print: Cut (1) 1" strip; Subcut
(16) 1" x 2" rectangles and (4) 1" squares.
White with green and yellow print #1: Cut (1) 1" strip;
subcut (16) 1" x 2" rectangles.
Red with white print: Cut (1) 1" strip; subcut (16) 1" x 2"
rectangles and (4) 1" squares.

This block is constructed by sewing horizontal rows.
Refer to the photograph of Jane's quilt for fabric placement. It is very important that you sew with an accurate
1/4" seam allowance.

Block #6:
6" x 6" finished (make 4)

Green with white print: Cut (2) 1" strips; subcut (1) 1" x
26" strip, (8) 1" squares and (16) 1" x 2" rectangles.
Cut (1) 1 1/2" strip; subcut (8) 1 1/2" x 1" rectangles,
(8) 1 1/2" x 2" rectangles. Cut (2) 3" strips; subcut (8)
3" x 4" rectangles and (8) 3" x 1 1/2" rectangles.
Yellow with white print: Cut (2) 1" strips; subcut (1) 1" x
26" strip and (16) 1" squares.
Red with white print: Cut (1) 1" strip; subcut (16) 1"
squares.

Sew the green with white print and yellow with white
print 26" strips together along the long edge and press
the seam allowance toward the green print. Cut the strip

set into (32) 1" segments. Refer to page 110 for instructions for making (16) 4-Patch units from the 1" segments.

Refer to the photograph of Jane's quilt. Notice that
the block is divided into 4 segments. Piecing the individual segments first will make completing the block much
easier.

PUTTING IT ALL TOGETHER
Refer to the "map" below. Arrange the blocks in the
order listed. Be sure that you also study the photograph
of Jane's quilt. Some blocks will need to be rotated. Sew
the 5 blocks of each row together, then sew the 5 rows
together to form the center of the quilt top.

6	4	5	4	6
4	3	2	3	4
5	2	1	2	5
4	3	2	3	4
6	4	5	4	6

BORDERS
Cut (4) 1 1/4" strips from the yellow with white and
green print. Measure the vertical center of the quilt top
and trim 2 of the strips to that measurement. Sew the
strips to the sides of the quilt top. Press the seam
allowance toward the strip.

Measure the horizontal center of the quilt top and
trim the remaining 2 strips to that measurement. Sew the
strips to the top and bottom of the quilt top. Press the
seam allowance toward the strip.

Cut (4) 4" strips from the white with green and yellow
print #2. Measure the vertical center of the quilt top and
trim 2 strips to that measurement. Sew the strips to the
sides. Press the seam allowance toward the strip.

Measure the horizontal center of the quilt top and
trim the remaining 2 strips to that measurement. Sew the
strips to the top and bottom. Press the seam allowance
toward the strip.

QUILTING
Jane machine quilted swirls and circles and filled in
space with a small meandering.

BINDING
Refer to page 122 for instructions for straight-edge
binding. Be sure to add a label to document your quilt!

Heart for Hope...

Heart for Tidings of Comfort

Add 1/4" seam allowance to fabric

Tidings of Comfort

58 3/4" x 58 3/4"
Made by Terry Pottmeyer of Mercer Island, Wash.

In Terry's quilt, words of comfort in the border, fabrics reminiscent of Grandma and the Comfort Quilt block combine to extend "tidings of comfort." Her goal was to make a vintage-looking quilt, so she combined the challenge fabrics with fabrics she recut from an old quilt top. All in all, this is a sweet quilt you will want to make!

FABRIC REQUIREMENTS

1/2 yard green solid (Comfort Quilt blocks)

1 1/2 yards green with white print (Comfort Quilt blocks, sashing, binding)

2 yards yellow with white and green print (Comfort Quilt blocks, sashing, border)

1 yard total assorted medium and light medium prints (Comfort Quilt blocks, cornerstones, appliqué hearts)

3 1/2 yards for backing

CUTTING INSTRUCTIONS

Green solid: Cut (3) 5 1/2" strips; subcut (36) 2 1/2" x 5 1/2" rectangles.

Green print with white print: Cut (4) 5 1/2" strips; subcut (64) 2 1/2" x 5 1/2" rectangles. Cut (3) 2 1/2" strips; subcut (64) 1 1/2" x 2 1/2" rectangles.

Yellow with white and green print: Cut (1) 5 1/2" strip; subcut (24) 1 1/2" x 5 1/2" rectangles. Cut (1) 7 1/2" strip; subcut (16) 7 1/2" rectangles.

Assorted prints: Cut 2 1/2" strips. (You will need at least 13 strips. You may use 13 different prints or a combination.) Subcut from the 2 1/2" strips (200) 2 1/2" squares. You will also need (41) 1 1/2" squares.

Refer to instructions for constructing the Comfort Quilt blocks on page 110. You will be making 25 blocks for this quilt that each measure 9 1/2" square (9" finished) if you sew with an accurate 1/4" seam allowance.

Use the solid green rectangles for 9 blocks and the green with white print for the remaining 16 blocks. Mix the assorted print 2 /12" squares in the blocks. Terry grouped the prints by color, using darker prints in the center of the blocks and lighter prints in the corners. Combined with the sashing, a secondary design is created.

When pressing your seams in putting the frames around the center 9-Patch, press away from the center 9-Patch.

SASHING

Sew a 1 1/2" x 2 1/2" green with white print rectangle to the end of a 7 1/2" yellow with white and green print rectangle. Press the seam allowance toward the longer piece.

Sew (2) 1 1/2" x 2 1/2" green with white print rectangles to both ends of a 5 1/2" yellow with white and green print rectangle. Press the seam allowances toward the longer piece.

PUTTING IT ALL TOGETHER

Look at the photograph of Terry's quilt. Notice the top and bottom rows: The blocks are separated by the first set of sashing pieces you made. The second, third and fourth rows show the blocks separated by the second set of sashing pieces.

The rows themselves are separated by rows of sashing pieces; each row begins and end with a sashing piece from the first set, while the second set of sashing pieces makes up the body of the sashing row. Each sashing piece in these rows is separated by a 1 1/2" square.

To put your quilt top together, construct the rows, then sew the rows together.

BORDER

Measure through the vertical center of your quilt top. If your 1/4" seam allowances are accurate, your quilt top probably measures about 49 1/2." Remove the selvage from the yellow with white and green print and cut from the length (2) 5 1/2" strips that are the length of your quilt top. Sew these strips to the sides.

Measure the horizontal center of the quilt top and cut (2) 5 1/2" strips that length. Sew these strips to the top and bottom.

Copy the heart template on page 67 28 times on the paper side of a paper-backed fusible web. Cut around the outside of the heart about 1/4"-1/2" and fuse the hearts to the wrong side of the assortment of prints.

Cut out the hearts on the line, peel the paper backing from the back and arrange on the border strips before sewing them to the quilt top. Choose a decorative stitch or the buttonhole stitch and machine stitch around each heart shape. Terry used a simple zigzag stitch.

You may add the hearts after the border strips are sewn to the quilt top, but the machine appliqué work is easier when working with just the strip. I usually make my strips a little longer, add the appliqué and then measure again and trim. Sometimes the appliqué work can draw the strip up a bit, altering the length.

QUILTING

Terry used a rainbow of pearl cotton threads to hand quilt a grid through the center of her quilt. She quilted a frame around the center and around each of the hearts; and she quilted words of comfort such as "hope," "dance," "hug" and "peace" between the appliquéd hearts.

BINDING

Refer to page 121-124 for directions for a straight-edge mitered binding. Terry finished her quilt with a heart-shaped label.

Hope . . .

36" x 37"
Made by Angie E. Purvis of Copperas Cove, Texas

Angie was inspired by the green prints from the Moda collection. She wanted to make a traditional-looking quilt and let the fabrics suggest a feeling of "hope for better times."

FABRIC REQUIREMENTS

1 fat quarter of 9 coordinating white with green and yellow prints, at least 4 "light" and 4 "dark"

1 fat quarter of solid green

1 1/4 yards white solid

1 1/8 yards for backing

BLOCK CONSTRUCTION

Fat quarter prints: Cut 4 template B shapes and 4 template C shapes.

White solid: Cut (1) 4 3/8" strip; subcut (8) 4 3/8" squares. Cut each square in half diagonally for (16) 1/2-square triangles.

Refer to page 113 for instructions in template piecing the Spider Web block. Make 4 blocks. (Angie made sure each fabric appeared in each of the 4 blocks in the same place for a controlled scrappy look.)

Sew the 4 blocks together for the center of the quilt top.

BORDER #1

White solid: Cut (4) 2" strips and (4) 4 1/2" strips.

Prints: Cut (2-3) 1 1/2" strips from of each print. They do not all have to be the same length. Sew the strips together, end to end, into (2) 28" strips and (2) 38" strips.

Measure the vertical center of your quilt top and trim (2) 2" white solid strips to that length. Sew the strips to the sides of your quilt top.

Measure the horizontal center of your quilt top and trim the remaining (2) 2" white solid strips to that length. Sew the strips to the top and bottom of your quilt top.

Sew the pieced strips from the print fabrics to each of the 4 1/2" white solid strips, along the long edges. Press the seam allowance toward the print strip so it does not shadow through the white fabric. (The pieced strip will not be as long as the white. You can trim the excess white.)

Measure the vertical center of your quilt top and trim the shorter pieced strip sets to that measurement. Sew the strip sets to the sides of your quilt top.

Measure the horizontal center of your quilt top; trim the remaining pieced strip sets to that measurement and sew them to the top and bottom of the quilt top.

APPLIQUÉ

Use your favorite appliqué method to add the vines and leaves to the quilt top. Angie hand appliquéd her design.

Green solid: Cut (6) 3/4" bias strips across the width of the fat quarter, each about 17". Make bias tape using a 3/8" Bias Tape. Trace 8 heart-shaped leaves, using the template on page 67, on the solid green fabric. Use these leaves to cover the ends of the bias tape.

Refer to the photograph of Angie's quilt and appliqué the bias tape to the quilt top.

Prints: Trace leaf #2 pattern on page 67 about 40 times on the assortment of prints. Refer to the photograph of Angie's quilt for placement.

Angie added color to her vine by stitching on floral shapes she found in one of the prints. You may do the same or use just leaves.

QUILTING

Angie hand quilted her work. She stitched 1/4" from the seams within the elements of the Spider Web blocks. She stitched around each of the appliqué shapes and quilted veins inside the leaves. A diagonal channel pattern finishes the border.

BINDING

Refer to page 122 for instructions on a straight binding.

Angie framed her label with random strips of the prints in her quilt top.

Maple Leaf Swirl

72" x 72"

Made by Jennifer S. Riggs of Walnut Creek, Calif. Quilted by Elaine Beattie.

Jennifer began with the Maple Leaf block and shifted the center dividing pieces. Doing so made the leaves appear to swirl around the block.

FABRIC REQUIREMENTS

2 1/4 yards yellow with white print (leaf background)

2 1/4 yards cream with red print #1 (leaf background)

1/8 yard each, for a total of 3 yards, 16-24 assorted prints (leaves)

1/3 yard white with red print #2 (border #1)

2 yards yellow with red and pink floral (border #2, border #3, binding)

1/2 yard pink with white print (border #2)

1/8 yard each, for a total of 1 1/2 yards, assorted white, green and yellow prints (border #4)

4 1/4 yard for backing

CUTTING INSTRUCTIONS

You will make a total of 16 blocks. For 8 you will use the yellow and white background print; for the other 8 you will use the cream with red background print.

Yellow and white background print: Cut (2) 6 1/2" strips; subcut (32) 2 1/2" x 6 1/2" rectangles. Cut (5) 2 1/2" strips; subcut (81) 2 1/2" squares. Cut (5) 3" strips; subcut (64) 3" squares. (For each of the 8 blocks you will need (9) 2 1/2" squares and (8) 3" squares.)

Cream with red background print: Cut (2) 6 1/2" strips; subcut (32) 2 1/2" x 6 1/2" rectangles. Cut (5) 2 1/2" strips; subcut (81) 2 1/2" squares. Cut (5) 3" strips; subcut (64) 3" squares. (For each of the 8 blocks you will need (9) 2 1/2" squares and (8) 3" squares.)

Assorted leaf prints: Cut (2) 3" squares and (3) 2 1/2" squares and make (1) 3" bias tape piece.

Pink with white print: Cut (6) 2" strips; subcut (120) 2" squares.

Yellow with pink and red floral: Cut (5) 3" strips; subcut (62) 3" squares. Cut each square in half diagonally, in both directions. You will have (248) 1/4-square triangles. Cut (8) 1 3/4" squares; cut each square in half diagonally.

Assorted green, yellow and white prints: Cut 3 1/2" strips; subcut (415) 1 1/2" x 3 1/2" rectangles.

CONSTRUCTING THE BLOCKS

Pair the 3" background squares and leaf fabric squares and make 1/2-square triangles units as described on page 29. After pressing the seam allowance toward the leaf fabric, trim the unit to measure 2 1/2" square.

Refer to the instructions for constructing the Maple Leaf units on page 112. To the top of each leaf unit, sew a 2 1/2" x 6 1/2" rectangle from the matching background fabric.

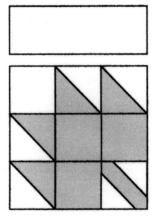

Four of these new units will be sewn to the 4 sides of the remaining 2 1/2" background square, using the "partial seam" technique.

Refer to the graphic below: Sew the 2 1/2" square to the leaf unit, beginning at the edge of the block and stopping about 1" from the end.

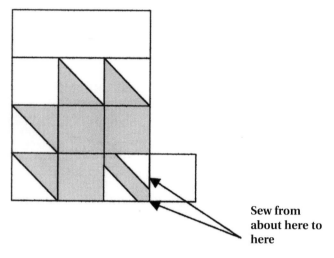

Sew from about here to here

To the left of the first leaf unit, sew another leaf unit, turning it a quarter-turn.

Keep adding leaf units, turning each a quarter-turn, until all 4 are attached around the center 2 1/2" square. Your final seam will complete the first seam and add the final leaf unit, completing the block.

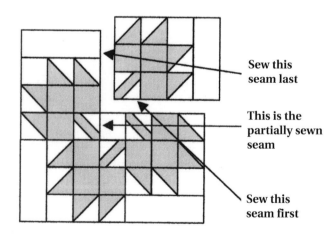

Sew this seam last

This is the partially sewn seam

Sew this seam first

Sew the 16 blocks together, alternating the backgrounds. Refer to the photograph of Jennifer's quilt for placement.

BORDER #1

Measure through the vertical center of your quilt top. Cut (8) 1 3/4" strips from the white with red print #2. Piece 2 strips together and trim to that measurement. Repeat with 2 more strips. Sew the strips to the sides.

Measure through the horizontal center of your quilt top. Piece 2 strips together and trim to the vertical measurement. Repeat with the remaining 2 strips, then sew them to the top and bottom.

BORDER #2

This border is a chain of "pearls." To all but 8 of the 2" pink with white squares, sew a 1/4-square triangle to 2 sides. The graphic below will show you the correct direction of the triangles.

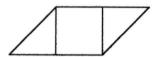

Sew (2) 1/2-square triangles to the remaining (8) 2" pink and white print squares, according to the graphic below. These are the "end" units.

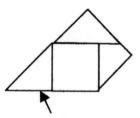

This is a 1/4-square triangle

Sew 26 "pearl" units together to form a strip. Note that the last "pearl" unit should not have a 1/4-square triangle. Sew a second strip in the same way. Sew an "end" unit to each end of the 2 strips. You should have 28 "pearls" in each strip. Sew these strips to the sides of your quilt top.

Sew 28 "pearl" units together to form a strip. Again, one 1/4-triangle unit will not be sewn on the ends. Sew a second strip in the same way. Sew the "end" units to each end of the strips. You will have 30 "pearls" in each strip; sew them to the top and bottom.

BORDER #3

Measure through the vertical center of your quilt top. Cut (8) 3" strips from the yellow with red and pink floral print. Piece 2 strips together and trim to that measurement. Repeat with 2 more strips. Sew the strips to the sides of your quilt top.

Measure through the horizontal center of your quilt top. Piece 2 strips together and trim to this measurement. Repeat with the remaining 2 strips. Sew the strips to the top and bottom of your quilt top.

BORDER #4

Jennifer created a braid for this final border. To begin, cut a 4 1/2" square from any scrap fabric you have and cut that diagonally in both directions. You will use these triangles as the base for each border strip, but eventually the triangles will be trimmed away.

Sew a green, yellow and white print 1 1/2" x 3 1/2" rectangle to one side of the triangle, aligning the 90-degree corners perfectly.

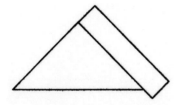

Add the next rectangle to the other side of the triangle, again aligning the 90-degree angles perfectly. Continue adding rectangles to alternating sides of the strip until it is the length you need. Measuring through the vertical center of the quilt will tell you how long to make the side strips. Measuring again through the horizontal center will give you the lengths of the top and bottom strip.

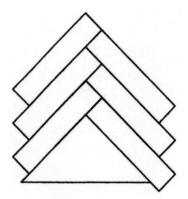

When you think you have added enough rectangles to the strips, add a few more. You will remove the end with the triangle so that you have nothing but the braid. Note, too, that by cutting the end of the strip on the angle instead of straight across, you will be able to miter the corners very easily.

A product that makes this so easy and accurate can be ordered from your local quilt shop. Ask for 2 rolls of 1 1/2" x 3" Sew and Fold paper from Triangles on a Roll. The paper is on a 150-foot roll and helps keep the braid straight.

QUILTING

Elaine quilted Jennifer's quilt by machine, working lovely swirling motifs in the Maple Leaf blocks and a swirling leafy vine in the braid border.

BINDING

Refer to page 122 for directions for making a straight-edged binding.

A label to document your quilt will finish the project.

'40s Comfort

41" x 41"
Made by Marilyn Robertson of Highland, Ind.

Marilyn says her goal was to re-create the look of the 1940s in this quilt.
She wanted it to be "comfortable" instead of showy.

FABRIC REQUIREMENTS

1/2 yard blue solid
Fat quarter each of 11 assorted medium and light prints
1/2 yard white solid
1/2 yard red solid
1 1/4 yard backing (if your fabric isn't 44" wide, you may have to piece the backing)

BLOCK CONSTRUCTION

Blue solid: Cut (6) 2 1/2" strips; subcut (20) 2 1/2" x 5 1/2" rectangles, (20) 2 1/2" x 1 1/2" rectangles, (32) 2 1/2" squares and (4) 1 1/2" squares.
Fat quarters: Cut (72) 2 1/2" x 5 1/2" rectangles (5-10 from each fat quarter), (16) 2 1/2" x 1 1/2" rectangles (4 each from 4 fat quarters), (40) 2 1/2" squares (4 each from 10 fat quarters), (5) 1 1/2" squares (1 each from 5 fat quarters).
White solid: Cut (3) 4" strips; subcut (26) 4" squares.
Red solid: Cut (8) 1 1/2" strips; set aside.

Refer to page 110 for instructions on constructing the Comfort Quilt block. You will make 5 blocks whose large rectangles are solid blue. You will make 4 blocks that have print in the large rectangles. Refer to the photograph of Marilyn's quilt for the placement of the prints you cut from the fat quarters.

Sew the 9 blocks together, alternating blue blocks with print. You will have 3 rows of 3 blocks.

BORDERS

Measure through the horizontal center of the quilt top. Trim (2) 1 1/2" red solid strips to this measurement and sew them to the top and bottom. Press the seam allowance toward the strip. (You will notice that this is the opposite of directions for other long horizontal borders. Marilyn used this orientation as a design element.)
Measure through the vertical center of the quilt top. Trim (2) 1 1/2" red solid strips to this measurement and sew them to the sides. Press the seam allowance toward the strip.
The second border is made by placing the assorted print rectangles "on point," that is, by sewing a triangle to each end, in opposite orientation, so the rectangles will slant.
Cut the white solid 4" squares diagonally in both directions.

Sew a triangle to the ends of the assorted rectangles. Refer to the graphic below.

Sew 2 rows of 12 rectangles together to form the top and bottom border strips. The graphic below will show you where to place the rectangles. Measure through the horizontal middle of the quilt top and trim the border strips to that measurement. Sew on the strips, pressing the seam allowance toward the red solid border strip.

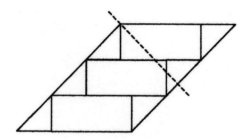

Sew 2 rows of 16 rectangles together to form the side border strips. Measure through the vertical center of the quilt top and trim the border strips to that measurement. Press the seam allowance toward the red solid border strip. Take care that you don't stretch the bias edges of the ends of the strips.

Once again, measure through the horizontal center of the quilt top and trim 2 red solid 1 1/2" strips to that measurement. Sew the strips to the top and bottom. Press the seam allowance toward the strip.

Measure through the vertical center of the quilt top and trim the remaining 2 red solid 1 1/2" strips to that measurement. Sew the strips to the sides. Press the seam allowance toward the strip.

QUILTING

Marilyn hand quilted a simple design that, as she says, suggests the quilt would have been used for comfort rather than for display.

BINDING

Marilyn cut strips from the remaining fat quarters and sewed them together to give her binding a "scrappy" look. Cut enough 2 1/2" strips to measure about 170 inches. Refer to page 122 for instructions in straight-edge binding.

Kansas City Star

61 1/2" x 61 1/2"
Made by Barbara A. Roidt of Jenera, Ohio, and quilted by Forever in Stitches of Bluffton, Ohio.

Barbara cleverly combined images of the Kansas City skyline with a beautiful rendition of Lone Star and Comfort Quilt blocks. Forever in Stitches worked a variety of quilting designs to enhance the piecing. You will love duplicating this quilt, which offers a variety of techniques to try!

FABRIC REQUIREMENTS

1/2 yard red solid (star and Comfort Quilt blocks – fabric #1

1/4 yard white floral on blue (star) – fabric #2

1/4 yard white with red and blue print #1 (star) – fabric #3

1/4 yard blue and white with red print (star) – fabric #4

7/8 yard yellow solid (star and binding) – fabric #5

1/4 yard blue with white print (star) – fabric #6

1/4 yard white with red and blue print #2 (star) – fabric #7

1/4 yard white with blue print (star) – fabric #8

1/8 yard medium blue solid (star) – fabric #9

1/2 yard white with red print (Comfort Quilt blocks)

1 3/8 yards blue with red and yellow floral print (border)

1 3/8 yards solid green (Cityscape)

1 3/8 yards white with green print (Cityscape)

1/2 yard white with navy print (corner blocks)

1/4 yard white with red and blue print #3 (corner blocks)

1/4 yard navy print (corner blocks)

3 1/2 yards backing fabric

LONE STAR POINTS

The Lone Star block is very satisfying to accomplish. Novice quilters may be intimidated, but if you to take it one step at a time you will be successful. You will have no problem if you stay organized and focused on accuracy. There are a variety of methods for accomplishing this block, but what I will describe has worked best for me. I'm sure it will work for you!

Refer to the grid in the graphic below. You will be making 5 strip sets using the fabrics listed. The numbers in the grid refer to the list of fabrics. Each star fabric in the Fabric Requirements list has a number that corresponds to the placement of the fabrics within the strip sets. If you stay organized, it really is easy!

Strip sets:

a	b	c	d	e
5	4	3	2	1
6	5	4	3	2
7	6	5	4	3
8	7	6	5	4
9	8	7	6	5

For each number in the grid you will need to cut (1) 1 3/4" strip. In other words, fabric #1 appears in only 1 space on the grid and only in strip set "e." You will need only 1 strip. Fabric #6 appears in 4 spaces on the grid, in strip sets "a," "b," "c" and "d." You will need to cut 4 strips from Fabric #6.

Once you have cut all the strips, stack them, right side up, into 5 stacks that represent the 5 strip sets. Start with the strip at the top of the column in the grid and add the 4 others in order. So, strip set "a" will have fabric #5 on top, followed by #6, #7, #8 and #9. Strip set "b" will have fabric #4 on top, followed by #5, #6, #7 and #8 and so on. As you create a strip set, pin the stack together at one end and label the strip set with its appropriate letter, a-e.

Accuracy is important when making this quilt. Before you begin making your strip sets, cut (3) 1 1/2" x 3 1/2" strips. Sew the strips together along the long edges, press the seams open and measure. The unit should measure 3 1/2" square. If it does, you may begin to sew the strip sets.

I highly recommend that if the unit does not measure 3 1/2" square you try again. You really need a 1/4" seam allowance to accomplish this quilt successfully. Something to remember: Your seam allowance should be a thread's width less than a true 1/4". You might have to disregard the 1/4" markings on your sewing machine.

Have you heard of the "scant" 1/4" seam allowance? This means the 1/4" seam allowance includes the sewn seam. So when measuring, include the thread. When determining where your needle should to be to create a 1/4" seam allowance, do not include it.

Once you have mastered the 1/4" seam allowance, you are ready to sew the strip sets. Trim the stack on one end, removing one selvage edge and creating a 45-degree angle. Refer to the graphic below.

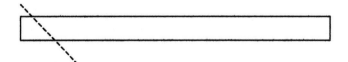

Begin with the first strip on your stack. Place the second strip on top of the first, right sides together, and sew together along the right side. Be careful that you don't turn your pair upside down.

Without rotating the strips, open the sewn strips and place the third strip on the second strip, right sides together. Again, sew the pair down the right side. Notice that you begin sewing the strip at the same end each time. Continue adding the strips until all 5 are sewn together. One side will be even and on a 45-degree angle and the other will be uneven but stair-stepped, depending on the various lengths of the strips. They will look like the graphic below.

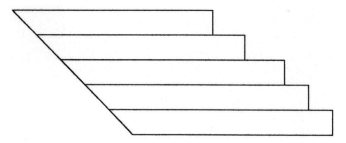

Carefully press the seam allowances open. Your pressing technique is extremely important here. You will be pressing, not "ironing." In other words, set the iron down and lift, move to the next spot and set the iron down and lift. You can move the tip of the iron through the seam allowance without actually contacting the ironing board. This lets you press the seam allowance open.

The important thing is that you do not stretch the strips. This will distort the strips, creating a "frown." Misting with spray starch also will help stabilize the fabric. In fact, I spray the starch and press two or three times.

Once the strip sets have been pressed, you will be ready to cut them into segments. Begin by straightening the first edge. Place a 6" x 24" rotary cutting ruler on the strip set so that the 45-degree line is aligned with one of the seams. The cutting edge should be as close as possible to the angled edge as you trim.

Cut a segment that measures 1 3/4" from the newly cut edge. Continue cutting until you have 8 segments. Between each cut, align the 45-degree line with the seam. Trim the angled edge between each segment you cut. This will ensure that your segments are as accurate as possible. Pin the segments into a stack and label with the strip set letter, i.e. strip set "a."

After cutting all the segments, stack them, right side up, into the 8 stacks that represent the star points. A segment from strip set "a" will be on top, followed by "b," "c," "d" and finally "e," all right side up. As you create a stack, carefully pin it together so as not to distort the fabric or disturb the bias edge. You will have 8 stacks.

Place the second segment in the stack on top of the first segment, right sides together, and place a pin at each of the intersecting seams. If you place a pin into the seam 1/4" from the raw edge of the segment on top, straight down through the seam 1/4" from the raw edge of the segment below, you will have aligned the seams perfectly. Place a second pin next to the first pin and pin as usual. Place a third pin on the other side of the first pin and pin as usual.

Once these two pins are placed, you may remove the

first pin. Repeat at each intersecting seam. Sew the seam, removing the pins as you reach them. Pick up the third segment and sew it to the right edge of the second, pinning at each intersecting seam. Repeat with each segment until you have sewn all 8 segments together into a star point. Set aside until all 8 star points are sewn, waiting to press them all at once.

Now that the star points are made, you'll want to make sure they all end up the same size and shape by blocking each unit. Measure through the center of several star-point units. If you have been consistent and accurate, they should all be relatively the same size. To make them all the exact same size, you'll begin with a guide.

I have tried this using freezer paper, but the steam pressing kept shrinking the paper and the star-point units ended up different sizes. I recommend that you draw your guide on a piece of prewashed muslin. Draw a straight line on the muslin with a permanent marker. Place the 45-degree line of the ruler on that line and draw another line, extending this line through the first one. This gives you two sides of the diamond.

Draw a line parallel to the first line using the measurement you determined when you measured through the center of the star-point units, again extending the line through the previous line. Using that same measurement, draw a line parallel to your second line, through the intersections. You will now have a guide to use when blocking all the diamond units.

Make a small dot in each corner, 1/4" in from the

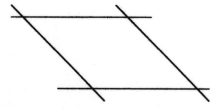

drawn line. Measure from dot to dot; if all is well, this measurement should be about 9 inches. This is the same as the finished measurement of the Comfort Quilt blocks. If the measurement is very different, you will have to adjust the size of the Comfort Quilt blocks and the Cityscape trapezoid pieces. See how important that accurate 1/4" seam allowance turned out to be?

Place a star-point unit on your guide, wrong side up. Pin the corners in place, aligning them with the drawn lines and placing the pins fairly flat. Pin the edges to the lines of your guide, stretching or easing where necessary. Be sure to use glass-head quilting pins so they won't melt while you press. With a steam iron, press the seams open. Remember, you are pressing, not ironing. The steam iron will help settle the fabric into the form so that each star-point unit will be the same shape and size. Let the unit cool a little before pulling the pins; set the unit aside so as not to stretch the bias edges.

On the wrong side of each star-point unit, mark the point 1/4" in from the raw edges at the corners. Set the star point units aside until you make the Comfort Quilt blocks.

COMFORT QUILT BLOCKS

Refer to instructions for constructing the Comfort Quilt blocks on page 110. You will be making 8 blocks for this quilt, using the red solid and white with red print. These blocks will measure 9 1/2" square (9" finished) if you sew with an accurate 1/4" seam allowance.

Red solid print: Cut (4) 2 1/2" strips; subcut (64) 2 1/2" squares. Cut (1) 1 1/2" strip; subcut (8) 1 1/2" squares.

White with red print: Cut (2) 5 1/2" strips; subcut (32) 2 1/2" x 5 1/2" rectangles. Cut (2) 2 1/2" strips; subcut (32) 1 1/2" x 2 1/2" rectangles.

On the wrong side of Comfort Quilt blocks, mark the point 1/4" in from the raw edges at the corners. The distance between marks should be 9" and should correspond to the distance between the marks you made on the star-point units.

CONSTRUCTING THE LONE STAR
AND COMFORT QUILT SETTING BLOCKS

To begin, you are going to pair 2 star-point units with 1 Comfort Quilt block. Set 4 Comfort Quilt blocks aside for now.

Matching the corner points that you noted 1/4" in from the raw edges, sew a star-point unit to the top of a Comfort Quilt block. Begin and end at the dots you marked and backstitch at each end. Note the placement of the units in the diagram below.

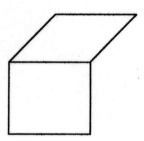

Matching the corner points that you noted 1/4" in from the raw edges, sew a star-point unit to the right side of a Comfort Quilt block. Again, begin and end at the dots you marked and backstitch at each end.

Sew the remaining seam, matching the intersecting seams as you did when you sewed the segments together to form the star-point units. I recommend you start sewing at the point of the 2 star-point units, beginning at the raw edge, and sew toward the 1/4" mark. Backstitch at the end of the seam.

Press the seams toward the Comfort Quilt block. Press the seam connecting the star points to one side. You may choose which direction to press the seam allowance, but the important thing is that each seam is pressed in the same direction each time. At this stage you will have four Y-seam units.

Next, sew 2 Y-seam units to a remaining Comfort Quilt block. As you did previously, sew a star-point unit edge to the top of a Comfort Quilt block. Begin and end

at the dots you marked and backstitch at each end. Sew a second Y-seam unit to the right side of the Comfort Quilt block, backstitching at the beginning and the end, stopping 1/4" from the corner edge.

The final seam will connect the star-point units, as you did when making the Y-seam unit. Again, you may sew through to the raw edge of the star-point unit. Press the seam allowances toward the Comfort Quilt block. The seam connecting the star points should be pressed in the same direction as the previous connecting seams.

Sew a remaining Comfort Quilt block to the right side of both units. This will create 2 halves of the Lone Star. For placement, refer to the diagram below.

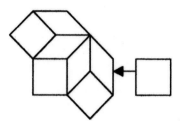

To sew the halves together, sew the star points to the Comfort Quilt blocks, beginning and ending with a backstitch at the mark 1/4" from the raw edge. Sew the seam connecting the star center last.

It is important that the center points all come together perfectly. To make this happen, begin sewing in the center and sew out to the edge in one direction and then repeat. You might want to sew just 1/2" or so in both directions from the center, just to make sure the center points all come together. It is easier to take apart a short seam than the entire seam. Remember to press the seam allowances all in the same direction around the center.

CITYSCAPE TRAPEZOID

Green solid: Cut (8) 7" x 22 1/2" rectangles.
White with green print: Cut (8) 7" x 22 1/2" rectangles.

Trace the Cityscape design A to the paper side of a lightweight paper-backed fusible web product of your choice. You need to trace the design 4 times. Repeat with Cityscape design B. Again, you need to trace the design 4 times.

Cut around the design about 1/2" from the outside of the line. Cut a window inside the design by cutting inside the line about 1/4" from the line. This keeps the appliqué from feeling overly stiff.

Fuse the paper templates to the wrong side of each white with green print rectangle. Cut on the drawn lines to create the Cityscapes. Peel the paper from the fabric and center the shapes, wrong side down, on the right side of the green solid rectangles, matching the raw edges along the bottom of the design. Following the manufacturer's instructions, fuse the fabric designs to the solid green pieces.

From the center of the bottom edge, measure 4 1/2" along the edge out toward an end and make a mark 1/4" in from the raw edge. Repeat in the opposite direction. These marks correspond to the distance between the marks you made on the Comfort Quilt blocks.

From the center of the top edge, measure 10 3/4" along the edge out toward an end and make a mark 1/4" from the raw edge. Repeat in the opposite direction.

If you lay your rotary cutting ruler on the rectangle so the 45-degree line is on a long edge of the rectangle and the 1/4" line is connecting the marks, you should be able to rotary cut the edges, making the trapezoid shape. Refer to the diagram below.

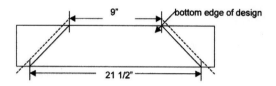

Sew the bottom edge of the Cityscapes to the Comfort Quilt block, beginning and ending at the marks 1/4" from the edges. Sew the end to the center Comfort Quilt block, beginning and ending at the marks. At the corners you will sew the ends of the green pieces, forming a mitered corner and sewing from the outer corner in toward the Comfort Quilt block. This will help avoid stretching the edges and distorting the corners. Refer to the picture of Barbara's quilt for clarification.

THE BORDER CORNER BLOCKS
According to Barbara Brackman's *Encyclopedia of Pieced Quilt Patterns*, the corner blocks are a variation of Kansas Star, which first appeared in *The Kansas City Star* in 1932.

White with navy print: Cut (2) 2 5/8" strips; subcut (16) 2 5/8" squares. Cut (3) 2 3/8" strips; subcut (40) 2 3/8" squares; cut each square in half diagonally once for (80) 1/2-square triangles.
White with red and blue print #3: Cut (2) 2 5/8" strips; subcut (20) 2 5/8" squares.
Navy print: Cut (2) 2 3/8" strips; subcut (32) 2 3/8" squares; cut each square in half diagonally once for (64) 1/2-square triangles.

To each white with red and blue print #3 square, sew 4 white with navy triangles. To each white with navy print square, sew 4 navy print triangles. Refer to the diagram below for the sewing sequence of the square-within-a-square units.

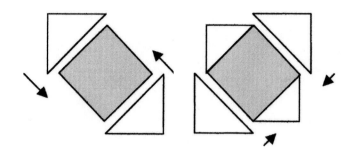

Each unit should measure 3 1/2" square. Look at Barbara's quilt and notice that each block takes 5 red and blue print squares and 4 white with navy squares. Arrange them according to the photograph and sew them together as you would a 9-Patch, 3 rows of 3 units each. Alternate the direction of the pressed seam allowances so that when you sew the rows together the seams butt up to one another.

Measure through the center of the quilt top in both directions. Remove the selvages from the blue with red and yellow floral print and cut (4) 9 1/2" strips from the length of the fabric. Cut these strips to the length that your quilt top measured. Sew 2 strips to the sides of the quilt top, pressing the seam allowance toward the border strip.

Sew a corner Kansas Star block to the ends of the remaining border strips. Press the seam allowance toward the border strip. Sew the border strips to the top and, again pressing the seam allowances toward the border.

QUILTING
The machine quilting includes straight-line quilting in the seams of the Lone Star and flowers over the Comfort Quilt blocks and the Kansas Star blocks. The border includes a stylized pattern reminiscent of the flowers in the border print.

BINDING
Refer to the directions on page 122 for straight-edge binding. A label will finish your quilt.

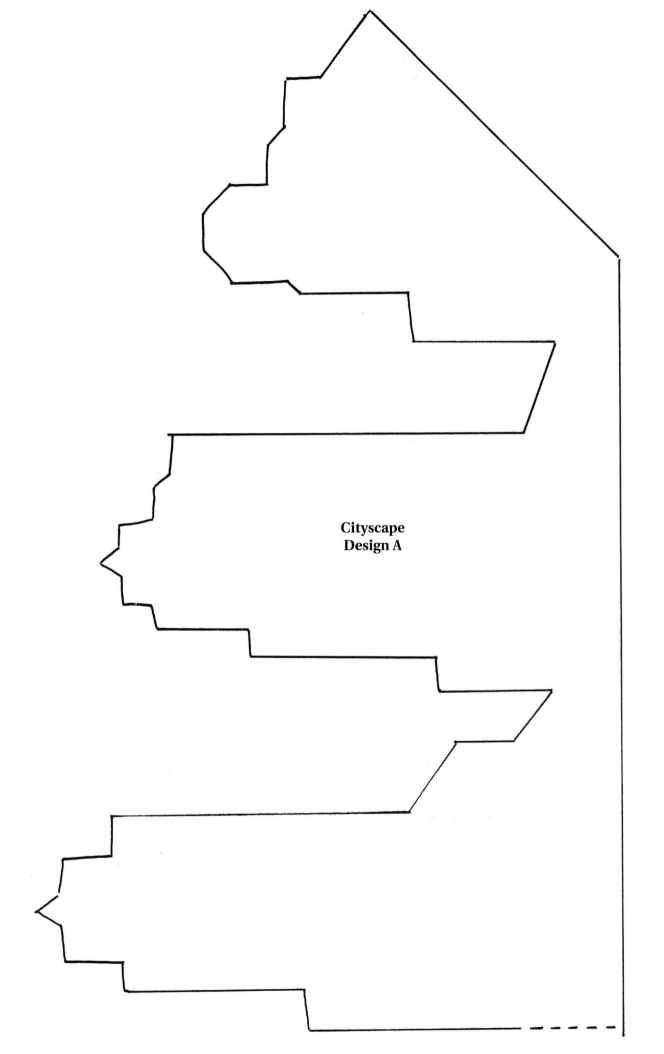

**Cityscape
Design A**

83

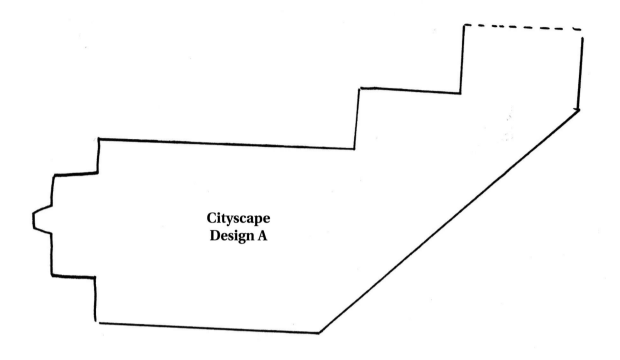

**Cityscape
Design A**

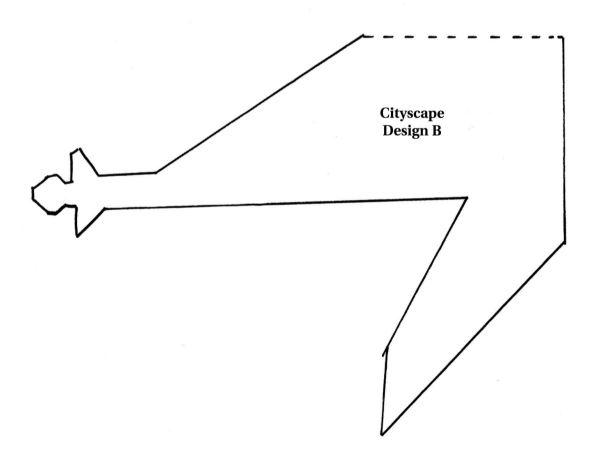

**Cityscape
Design B**

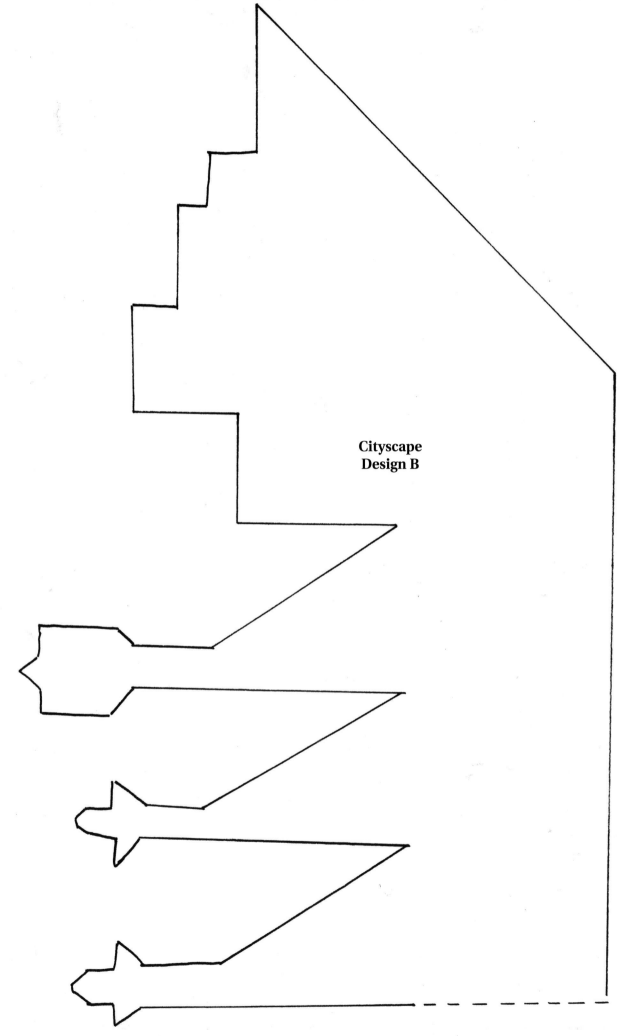

**Cityscape
Design B**

85

Sunshine on Ruby's Tulips

44" x 44"
Made by Nancy Romine of Emporia, Kan.

Nancy fashioned the tulips in her quilt after a pattern in the "Designs Worth Doing" catalog from the McKim studios. Nancy says she foundation pieced the tulips but made each one different by "crazy piecing" the petals, using from 3 to 12 pieces in the flowers. So get your creative juices flowing and have fun with these tulips!

FABRIC REQUIREMENTS

5/8 yard yellow solid (inner border, binding)
1/3 yard yellow with white print (spikes, template B pieces, 4-Patch units, Dogwood Blossom block frame)
1/4 yard white with yellow print (4-Patch units, template B pieces)
1 5/8 yards blue with white print (spike background, template C pieces, tulip block background)
1/8 yard red solid (Dogwood Blossom block frame)
1/8 yard each, variety of green prints (tulip leaves and stems)
1/8 yard each, variety of yellow, pink, and red floral prints (tulips)
1 1/4 yards red print (outer border)
48-50" square backing (you will probably have to piece it unless you use an extra-wide fabric)

BLOCK CONSTRUCTION

Nancy's quilt has only one Dogwood Blossom block, which she meant to represent sunshine. You will need 8 copies of the arc foundation. Refer to page 119 for directions on Paper Foundation Piecing.

Dogwood Blossom Block

4-Patch Units

Yellow with white print: Cut (1) 2" strip
White with yellow print: Cut (1) 2" strip.

Refer to page 116 for directions for sewing the strips together. Press the seam allowances toward the yellow with white print. Cut the strip set into (16) 2" x 3 1/2" segments. Pair 2 segments, inverting 1, and sew together, matching the intersecting seam. You should have (8) 3 1/2" square 4-Patch units.

Arc Units

Yellow with white print: Cut (1) 2 1/2" strip; subcut to (40) 1" x 2 1/2" rectangles for the spikes.
Blue with white print: Cut (2) 2 1/2" strips; subcut to (32) 2" x 2 1/2" rectangles for the spike backgrounds.

Foundation piece the 8 arc units according to the directions on page 114.

Yellow with white print: Cut 4 template B pieces.
White with yellow print: Cut 4 template B pieces.

Blue with white print: Cut 8 template C pieces.

Sew the template B and C pieces to the arc units. You should have (8) 3 /12" square arc units.

Look at Nancy's quilt for placement and orientation of 4-Patch units and arc units. Your Dogwood Blossom block should measure 12 1/2" square.

Tulip Blocks

Nancy's quilt has 16 tulips; 8 have longer stem and leaves, and 8 have shorter stems and leaves. You will need 16 copies of the tulip foundation pattern and 8 each of the leaf foundation patterns. The technique for foundation piecing the tulip units is the same as for the arc units. Just remember that the numbers are your sewing sequence.

Green prints: Cut (8) 1" x 7" strips for long stems and (8) 1" x 4" strips for short stems. Cut (16) 1 3/4" x 6" rectangles for long leaves and (16) 1 1/2" x 2 1/2" rectangles for short leaves.
Yellow, pink and red floral prints: Cut 2 1/2" strips; subcut some pieces to 4 1/2", some to 2 1/2" and some to 2" if you don't plan to crazy piece the tulips.
Blue with white print: Cut (1) 3 1/2" strip; subcut to (8) 3 1/2" x 3 3/4" rectangles for corner tulips. Cut (1) 8 1/4" strip; subcut to (4) 8 1/4" squares. Cut each square in half on the diagonal. You will have (8) 1/2-square triangles for the corner blocks. Cut (1) 9 1/2" strip; subcut to (16) 2" x 9 1/2" rectangles for spacers between the tulip blocks.

Refer to the foundation piecing instructions on page 114. Remember to have some fun with the tulips and add as many extra fabrics as you like. All you have to do is break each of the patches into additional strips.

PUTTING IT ALL TOGETHER

Red solid: Cut (4) 3/4" strips; subcut the strips to (2) 3/4" x 12 1/2" pieces, (2) 3/4" x 13" pieces, (2) 3/4" x 14 1/2" pieces and (2) 3/4" x 15 1/2" pieces.
Yellow with white print: Cut (2) 1 1/2" strips; subcut to (2) 1 1/2" x 13" pieces and (2) 1 1/2" x 14 1/2" pieces.

To frame the Dogwood block, sew a 3/4" x 12 1/2" red strip to the sides of the block and press the seam allowances toward the strip. Sew a 3/4" x 13" red strip to

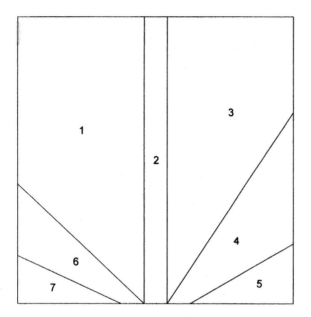

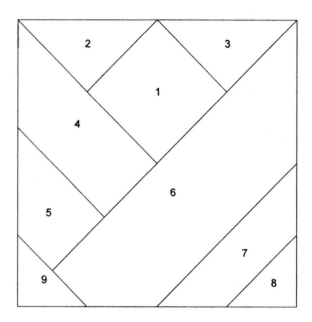

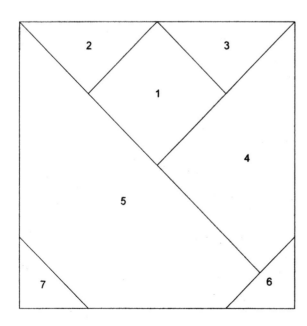

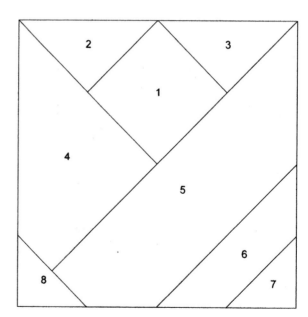

the top and bottom of the block and press toward the strip.

Sew a 1 1/2" x 13" yellow strip to the sides of the block and press the seams toward the strip. Sew a 1 1/2" x 14 1/2" strip to the top and bottom of the block, pressing the seam allowance toward the strip.

Sew a 3/4" x 14 1/2" red strip to the sides of the block and press the seams toward the strip. Sew a 3/4" x 15 1/2" red strip to the top and bottom of the block and press the seam toward the strip.

Sew a tulip block to each leaf block. To 4 of the 6" flower units, sew a 3" x 3 1/4" blue with white print rectangle to the top of the tulip.

Look at Nancy's quilt. You will make 4 tulip strips that fit on the sides of the center framed block. Each tulip strip begins and ends with a 2" x 9 1/2" blue with white print strip. Each tulip unit is separated from the next by a 2" x 9 1/2" blue and white print strip. Sew 1 tulip strip to each side of the center framed block. Press the seam allowances toward the center framed block.

Sew a blue with white print 3 1/2" x 4" rectangle to the top and bottom of the remaining (4) 6" tulip units. Find and mark the center of the long sides of the tulip blocks. Find and mark the center of the long side of the blue with white print 1/2-square triangles. Match the center point and sew the triangles to the long side of the tulip block. Press the seam allowance toward the triangle. Repeat with a second triangle on the opposite side of the tulip block. Trim the block to 9 1/2" square. Make 4 of these corner blocks.

Sew a corner block to the ends of the remaining tulip strips. Press the seam allowance toward the corner blocks. Sew the tulip strips to the top and bottom of the center framed block. Press the seam allowance toward the center framed block.

BORDERS

Cut (4) 2" yellow solid strips for the inner borders. Measure through the vertical center of the quilt top and trim 2 strips to that measurement. Sew the strips to the sides of the quilt top. Press the seam allowanced toward the border strips.

Measure through the horizontal middle of the quilt top and trim the 2 remaining strips to that length. Sew the strips to the top and bottom of the quilt top. Press the seam allowances toward the borders strips.

Remove the selvages and cut the 4 1/2" outer border strips from the length of the fabric. Press the seam allowances toward the outer border.

QUILTING

Nancy machine quilted cross-hatching in the center and, around all the flowers and repeated a motif in the outer border and corner tulip blocks.

BINDING

Refer to the instructions for straight binding on beginning on page 122.
Don't forget to make a label for your quilt.

Sunshine Patterns
Leaves and stems

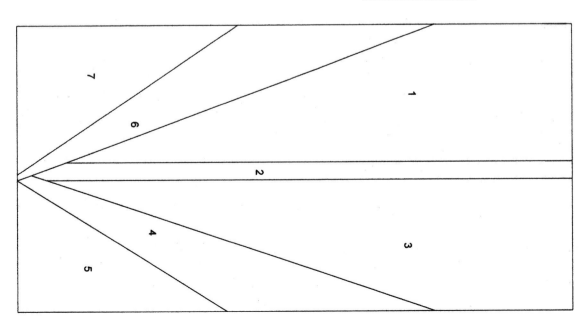

Spring in Bloom

55 1/4" x 55 1/4"
Made by Wendy Sticken of Creston, Iowa.

The focus of Wendy's quilt is the Eight-Point Star.
Barbara Brackman's "Encyclopedia of Pieced Blocks" credits Ruby McKim with this
block, so it is very fitting that Wendy's quilt is built around it. By judicious placement of color
and dimensional prairie points, Wendy has turned this star into a blossom.

FABRIC REQUIREMENTS

1/4 yard light pink print
1/4 yard dark pink print (this can still be "light" but must be darker than the first pink; it may be solid instead)
1/4 yard light lavender print
1/4 yard dark lavender print (same as the dark pink print)
1/4 yard light yellow print
1/4 yard dark yellow print (same as the dark pink print)
(Note: You may use more than 6 prints if you like.)
1 fat quarter solid green
2 1/3 yards white background
1/2 yard pastel floral print #1 (Little Cedar Tree blocks)
1/2 yard pastel floral print #2 (Little Cedar Tree blocks)
1 1/2 yards pastel blue (borders and binding)
3 1/3 yards (backing)

EIGHT-POINT STAR BLOCKS
AND BORDER TULIP BLOCKS
CUTTING INSTRUCTIONS

Light and dark pink, lavender and yellow prints: Cut (3) 2 1/2" strips from each; subcut (24) 2 1/2" wide 45-degree diamonds from the pink and lavender fabrics. Subcut (26) 2 1/2" wide 45-degree diamonds from the two yellow prints. Cut (13) 2 1/2" squares from the dark pink print, (12) 2 1/2" squares from the dark lavender print, (12) 2 1/2" squares from the dark yellow print.

Green solid: Cut (1) 2 1/2" strip; subcut (6) 2 1/2" wide 45-degree diamonds. Cut (3) 2" strips; subcut (56) 2" squares. Cut (1) 4" square. Cut (2) 1" x 14" strips; subcut (2) 1" x 7" strips.

White background: Cut (1) 5" strip; subcut (3) 5" squares. Cut each square in half diagonally in both directions for (12) 1/4-square triangles. Cut (3) 5" strips; subcut (56) 2" x 5" rectangles. Cut (4) 3" strips; subcut (49) 3" squares. Cut (2) 2" strips; subcut (28) 2" squares. Cut (1) 9 1/2" square. Cut (4) 2 1/2" strips; subcut (37) 2 1/2" squares. Cut the squares in half diagonally for (74) 1/2-square triangles. Cut (1) 1" x 6 1/2" strip; subcut (28) 1" x 6 1/2" rectangles.

Pastel blue solid: Cut (4) 2 1/4" strips. Cut (10) 2 1/2" strips.

CONSTRUCTING THE EIGHT-POINT STAR BLOCKS

Pair the light diamonds with dark diamonds and sew the pairs of diamonds together. Stop sewing 1/4" from the V end of each pairing. Sew 3 pairs of green diamonds in the same way. Press the seams open.

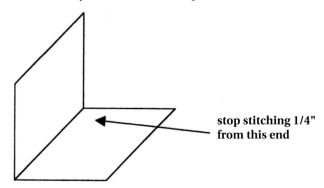

stop stitching 1/4" from this end

For each of the 3 Eight-Point Star blocks you will need 3 pairs of print diamonds of one color, 1 pair of green diamonds and (7) 2 1/2" squares (lavender for the pink diamond star, pink for the yellow star and yellow for the lavender star). You will need (4) 1/4-square triangles and (4) 3" squares of the background fabric.

Fold the 2 1/2" squares in half diagonally. You will have a triangle consisting of (2) 45-degree angles and (1) 90-degree angle. Fold the 45-degree corners to the 90-degree corner to form the bud. Secure the folds by sewing 1/8" from the raw edge or pinning the folds. Pin the bud to the 90-degree corner of each of the 1/4-square triangles and to one corner of the each of the squares.

Sew the 4 pairs of diamonds to the 1/4-square triangles, sewing from the points toward the 90-degree angle. Press the seam allowances away from the background 1/4-square triangle. Sew a background square to the right petal, making sure the prairie point bud is toward the center of the block. You should have 4 units.

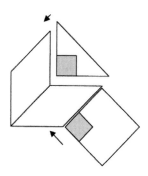

Sew 2 star units together, matching the petals in the center. Sew from the corner of the prairie point into the center of the star, then from the corner of the prairie point out to the block's edge. Now you have 2 halves of the block.

Sew the final star point to a background square, sewing out toward the edge of the block. Your final seam is across the center. I suggest beginning at the center point and sewing toward the square, then from the center point toward the opposite background square.

Press the seams of the star open. Press the seams of the corner squares and 1/4-square triangles toward the star.

Sew the Eight-Point Stars and the 9 1/2" background square together, referring to the photograph of Wendy's quilt for placement.

Fold each green solid 1" strip into thirds, overlapping to create 3/8" strips. Release a few stitches in the inner V created by the green diamonds in the center star and tuck the end of the strip in, folded side down. Restitch the inside corner, catching the strip.

Repeat with the 1" x 7" strips, tucking them into the inner V of the green diamonds of the side stars. Restitch the inside corners, catching the strips.

Tuck the ends of the shorter strips under the longer strip. The longer strips should be placed diagonally across the 9 1/2" background square. Machine stitch the strips to the block. Wendy used a small buttonhole stitch on both sides of the strips, securing them to the block.

Place the 4-inch green square over the free corner of the 9 1/2" background square. Draw a line diagonally across the square and sew on the line. Fold the square over the stitching, matching the corners. Trim the middle layer. (Leaving the background square intact lets you maintain the accuracy of your square.)

Using your favorite method, appliqué the leaves to the block, using the template for the leaves on page 93 and referring to the photograph of Wendy's quilt for placement. Wendy used the fusible appliqué method and repeated the machine buttonhole stitch to secure the leaves to the background.

Sew the (4) 2 1/2" background strips to the (4) 2 1/4" blue solid strips along the long edge. Press the seam allowance toward the blue fabric strips. Following the instructions on page 121 for a mitered border, sew the strip set to the starflower block. The white strip is sewn to the flower block, while the blue strip frames it all.

CONSTRUCTING THE LITTLE CEDAR TREE BLOCKS

Each corner unit is made from (9) 3-inch finished floral #1 blocks, (6) 3-inch finished floral #2 blocks and (6) 1/2-square triangles cut from 3 7/8" squares. This means (72) 2 3/8" squares of floral #1 and (48) 2 3/8" squares of floral #2 and an equal number of background squares. (Using a product from your local quilt shop that is designed for making lots of 1 1/2" finished 1/2-square triangle units makes this go much quicker.)

Refer to the photograph of Wendy's quilt for placement and sew the rows of Little Cedar Tree blocks together, ending each row with a 1/2-square triangle. A single 1/2-square triangle will finish the large triangle unit. Sew the 4 units to the sides.

Measure through the vertical center of the quilt top and trim (2) 2 1/2" blue strips to that length. Sew the strips to the sides of the quilt top. Measure through the horizontal center of the quilt top and trim (2) 2 1/2" strips to that measurement. Sew these strips to the top and bottom.

CONSTRUCTING THE TULIP BORDER

Make the dimensional prairie points and sew or pin them to a corner of the remaining 3" background squares. Inset the squares into a pair of diamonds in the same way you inserted the 1/4-square triangles in the Eight-Point Star blocks. Sew a 2 1/2" 1/2-square triangle to complete the tulip bud.

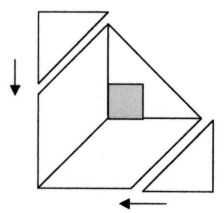

Place a 2" green square on one end of each of the 2" x 5" background rectangles. Sew diagonally across the triangle as the diagram below shows.

Fold the square over the stitching, matching the corner. Press and remove the center layer of fabric.

Sew a 2" square of background fabric to half of the 2" x 5" rectangles on the end with the green triangle.

Sew a 2" x 5" rectangle with green triangle to the left side of the bud. Sew a rectangle that includes the background square on the end to the bottom of the bud to complete the block. You will have 37 tulip bud blocks.

Sew 6 tulip bud blocks together in a row, separating each block with a 1" x 6 1/2" rectangle. Alternate the orientation of each tulip block so they look as if they are tumbling around the quilt. Refer to the photograph of Wendy's for placement. Make 2 rows.

Sew a 1" x 6 1/2" strip to each end of the row and sew the rows to the sides of your quilt top.

Sew 8 tulip blocks together in a row, separating each block with a 1" x 6 1/2" rectangle. Again, alternate the orientation. Make 2 rows and sew these to the top and bottom.

FINAL BORDER

You should have (6) 2 1/2" blue strips remaining. Cut 2 strips in half so they measure about 2 1/2" x 20." Sew a short strip to each long strip, end to end.

Measure the sides of the quilt top and trim the strips to fit it; sew the strips to the sides and press the seam allowances toward the strips. Repeat for the top and bottom.

QUILTING

Wendy machine quilted plenty of swirls and curls and even added a leafy vine in the blue strips.

BINDING

Refer to page 122 for instructions on straight binding.

Wendy made her label by embroidering her information on fabric. She even used the same colors in the thread that appear on the front of the quilt.

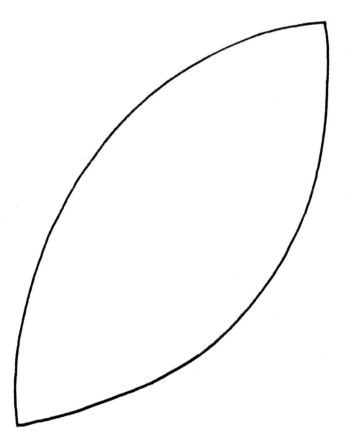

**Leaf for
Spring in Bloom**

Red Paintbrush
42" x 42"
Made by Marlys Tillman of Salina, Kan.

Marlys' entry form for the Challenge was accompanied by a photograph of a meadow full of blooming Great Red Paintbrush and splashes of yellow, creamy white and pink. Her cheerful quilt puts the viewer in that meadow!

FABRIC REQUIREMENTS

5/8 yard green with white print (Little Cedar Tree blocks, stems)

1/2 yard white with green print (Little Cedar Tree blocks)

5/8 yard white with green and yellow print (leaves, flower center, binding)

1/4 yard yellow with white print (flower head)

1/8 yard red solid (flower petals, border #1)

1/8 yard red with white print (flower petals)

1 1/8 yards white solid (flower background)

5/8 yard green with white and yellow print (border #2)

1 1/3 yards backing

CUTTING INSTRUCTIONS

Green with white print: Cut (3) 4 3/8" strips; subcut (24) 4 3/8" squares. Cut (4) 4" squares.

White with green print: Cut (3) 4 3/8" strips; subcut (24) 4 3/8" squares.

White solid: Cut (3) 4 3/8" strips; subcut (22) 4 3/8" squares. Cut (13) 4 3/8" squares in half diagonally for (26) 1/2-square triangles. Cut (2) 7 3/8" strips; subcut (7) 7 3/8" squares. Cut the 7 3/8" squares in half diagonally for (14) 1/2-square triangles. You will use 13.

Yellow with white print: Cut (1) 4 3/8" strip; subcut (8) 4 3/8" squares. Cut (1) 4 3/8" square.

Green with white and yellow print: Cut (4) 4" strips.

LITTLE CEDAR TREE BLOCKS

Refer to page 111 for instructions on constructing the Little Cedar Tree blocks. Make a total of 12.

PAINTBRUSH BLOCKS

Following instructions on page 29, make (17) 1/2-square triangle units from 9 white solid 4 3/8" squares and 9 yellow with white print 4 3/8" squares.

Use your favorite method to appliqué the flower petals and centers cut from templates of page 96. Marlys fused her appliqués and used the buttonhole stitch on her sewing machine and a matching thread to secure them. For each block you will need 3 petals from the red solid and 2 from the red with white print.

Make 13 stems using to your favorite appliqué method; the template is presented for fusible appliqué. The stems will be sewn into the seam allowance before fusing or stitching. Notice on Marlys' quilt that 7 stems curve down from right to left and 6 stems curve up from left to right. That means 7 stems are tucked into the seam allowance on the left of the yellow triangle and 6 are tucked into the seam allowance on the right. Be sure to place the side of the stem 1/4" from the edge so it will be free to fold over when the seams are stitched.

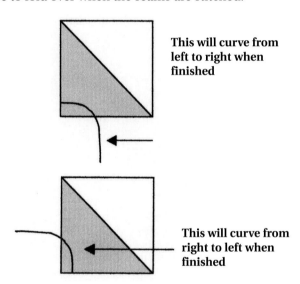

This will curve from left to right when finished

This will curve from right to left when finished

Sew the smaller white solid triangles to the sides of the yellow with white triangles, forming a larger triangle.

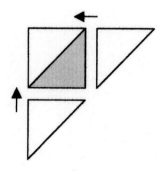

Sew the larger white triangles to the appliqué triangles to form the Paintbrush blocks. Avoid catching the stem in the seam. Open out the block and press the seam allowance toward the larger triangle. Complete the stem by stitching it to the larger triangle. Add the large leaf to each block. Refer to the photograph of Marlys' quilt for placement.

**Red Paintbrush
Templates**

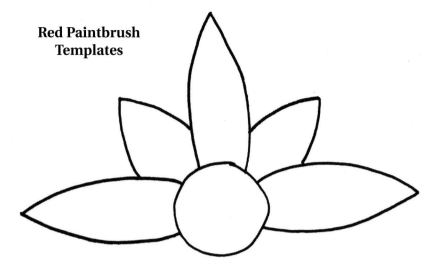

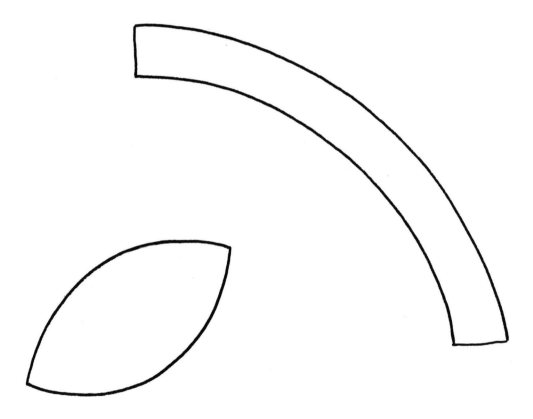

Add 1/4" seam allowance to fabric

PUTTING IT ALL TOGETHER

Refer to the photograph of Marlys' quilt to arrange your blocks. Remember that the stems alternate directions across the quilt.

Border #1

I have used this 1/8" touch of color next to a binding. It is amazing how dramatic the tiny sliver of fabric becomes!

Cut (4) 5/8" strips of red solid fabric. Sew the strips to the edge of the quilt top, using a 1/4" seam allowance. Press the seam allowance toward the strip, which will take extra care as the strip is so thin. When you add the next border, sew with your usual 1/4" seam; you will end up with a sliver of color and you won't be cutting off any points as you would with a flange.

Border #2

Measure through the vertical center of the quilt top. Trim (2) 4" green with white and yellow print strips to that measurement. Place a green with white 4" square on each end of the strips and sew a line diagonally through the square, as shown in the graphic below.

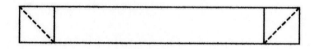

Fold the triangle back and press. Trim the center layer of fabric away 1/4" from the seam. Remove only the center layer.

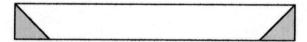

Sew the strips to the sides of the quilt top with a 1/4" seam allowance. Press the seam allowance toward the strip. You should have a mere 1/8" sliver of solid red between the quilt top and the border strip.

Measure through the horizontal center of the quilt top. Trim the remaining (2) 4" strips to that measurement. Sew the remaining green with white print squares as you did the side border strips. Sew the remaining Paintbrush appliqué units to the ends and press the seam allowance toward the strips.

Sew the strips to the top and bottom of your quilt top with a 1/4" seam allowance and press the seam allowance toward the strip.

QUILTING

Marlys used her sewing machine to stitch "in the ditch" in the Little Cedar Tree blocks, defining the squares in the 4-Patch. She stitched around each Paintbrush flower and finished with a straight channel of stitching in the border strips between the corner flowers.

BINDING

Refer to page 122 for instructions on straight-edged binding.

On her label, Marlys documented everything from the purpose for making the quilt to its inspiration and the methods she used to make it. Posterity will have no questions about this quilt!

Dogwood Do Si Do

39" x 39"

Made by Annie Unrein of St. George, Utah.

*Annie says her quilt reminds her of square dancing with its
swirling skirts and intricate footwork.
The 4-Patch units that form the chains
across the quilt represent the measured steps in the dance.*

Annie says she can just hear the caller singing, "Swing your partner! Do si do!" Annie notes that another name for the Dogwood Blossom block is Suspension Bridge and that her quilt forms a bridge between the historical block and her interpretation. For more designs and patterns by Annie Unrein, please visit her Website, www.byannie.com.

Refer to the resized Dogwood Blossom block patterns on pages 131-135. You will need to make templates for B and C in both sizes. You will need 8 copies of the smaller and 8 copies of the larger foundation for paper piecing. Piece A will be rotary cut and strip pieced according to the directions on page 113.

FABRIC REQUIREMENTS
1/3 yard light pink print (4-Patch units, center variable 9-Patch)
1/2 yard medium pink print (spikes, inner border)
5/8 yard dark pink print (spikes, binding)
1/4 yard lime solid (4-Patch units, center variable 9-Patch)
1/2 yard lime print (double 4-Patch blocks, B templates, C templates)
1 1/4 yards pink floral print (spike background, outer border)
1 1/4 yards for backing

CONSTRUCTING THE UNITS
4-Patch Units
Refer to page 116 for directions in making 4-Patch units. Each unit, when complete, should measure 4 1/4" square

Light pink print: Cut (2) 2 3/8" strips. Cut 1 strip into 2 pieces, each 20 inches long. Cut (1) 20-inch strip into (4) 2 3/8-inch squares. Cut a 4 1/4" square from the remainder of the light pink print.

Lime solid: Cut (2) 2 3/8" strips. Cut 1 strip into 2 pieces, each 20 inches long. Cut (1) 20-inch strip into (4) 2 3/8" x 4 1/2" rectangles

Lime print: Cut (1) 4 1/4" strip; subcut (8) 4 1/4" squares.

Sew 1 pink 20" strip to 1 lime 20" strip. Sew the pink 40-inch and lime 40-inch strips together. Press the seam allowances toward the lime. Subcut the strips into (24) 2 3/8" segments.
Pairing (2) 2 3/8" segments, invert 1 and sew them together, creating the 4-Patch units. You will need (12) 4-Patch units.

Set aside (4) 4-Patch units. Sew the remaining (8) 4-Patch units to the (8) 4 1/4" squares. Treat these new units as you did the segments cut from the strip sets. Pair 2, inverting 1, and sew the 2 segments together, creating a Double 4-Patch block. You will have a total of 4 Double 4-Patch blocks that measure 8" square.

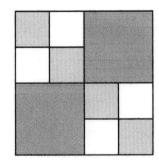

Arc Units

Refer to page 119 for instructions on Paper Foundation Piecing. You will need a total of 8 arcs from each sized pattern included here. Refer to the photograph of Annie's quilt for color placement in the arc units.

Medium pink print: Cut (3) 2" strips; subcut to (24) 2" x 4 1/4" rectangles for the large arc unit spikes. Cut (1) 2 1/2" strip; subcut to (24) 1 1/4" x 2 1/2" rectangles for the small arc unit spikes.

Dark pink print: Cut (1) 4 1/2" strip; subcut to (16) 2" x 4 1/2" rectangles for the large arc unit spikes. Cut (1) 2 1/2" strip; subcut to (16) 1 1/4" x 2 1/2" rectangles for the small arc unit spikes.

Pink floral print: Cut (3) 4" strips; Subcut to (32) 3 1/2" x 4" rectangles for the large arc unit spike backgrounds. Cut (2) 2 1/2" strips; subcut to (32) 2" x 2 1/2" rectangles for the small arc unit spike backgrounds.

Templates B and C

Cut 8 large template B pieces and 8 small template B pieces from the lime print. Sew a template B pieces to each of the 8 arc units in each size.

Cut 8 large template C pieces and 8 small template C pieces from the lime print. Sew a template C pieces to each of the 8 arc units in each size.

Center Variable 9-Patch Block

To eliminate bulky seams, Annie transformed (4) 4-Patch units into a single Variable 9-Patch block.

Sew a 2 3/8" light pink square to either end of (2) 2 3/8" x 4 1/4" lime solid rectangles. Sew a 2 3/8" x 4 1/4" lime solid rectangle to either side of the 4 1/4" light pink square. Following the layout in the graphic below, sew the 3 rows together. The Variable 9-Patch block should measure 8" square.

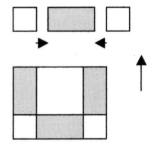

Joining the Blocks

The center of Annie's quilt is put together with the 8 smaller arc units, the (4) 4-Patch units you set aside and the Variable 9-Patch block. Refer to the photograph for placement and orientation of the units. The large arc units and Double 4-Patch block are arranged to surround the center. Again, refer to the photograph of Annie's quilt for placement.

BORDERS

For the inner border, cut (4) 1" strips from the medium pink print.

For the outer border, cut (4) 4/1/4" strips from the pink floral print.

Measure through the vertical center of the quilt top and trim 2 strips to fit. Match the center of the strips to the center of the sides of the quilt top and sew the strips, pressing the seam allowances toward the outer border strips.

Measure through the horizontal center of the quilt top and trim the remaining 2 strips to fit. Match the center of the strips to the center of the top and bottom of the quilt top and sew the strips, pressing the seam allowances toward the outer border strips.

QUILTING

Annie used hand and machine quilting. She used the machine to stitch around each of the spikes and to add a meandering design in the spike backgrounds. Her hand quilting designs included cross-hatching and clamshells. You should feel free to be creative and add your own touch.

BINDING

Refer to page 122 for instructions in straight binding.

Don't forget to make a label when you complete your quilt!

Shaker Tree
55 1/2" x 70"
Made by Kimberly Weingart of Hiram, Ohio.

Kimberly's quilt is very graphic because of her use of solid red, blue and green. The coordinating prints make the solid fabrics "pop"!

FABRIC REQUIREMENTS

5/8 yard green solid (blocks and cornerstones)
1/8 yard white with green print (blocks)
1/8 yard green with white and yellow print #1 (blocks)
1/8 yard white with yellow and green print (blocks)
1/8 yard green with white and yellow print #2 (blocks)
5/8 yard red solid (blocks and cornerstones)
1/8 yard red with white and blue print (blocks)
1/4 yard white with red and blue print #1 (blocks)
1/8 yard white with red and blue print #2 (blocks)
1/8 yard white with red print (blocks)
1 3/4 yards blue solid (blocks, cornerstones, border)
1/8 yard white with blue print (blocks)
1/8 yard white with blue and red print #1 (blocks)
1/8 yard white with blue and red print #2 (blocks)
1/2 yard white with red and blue floral print (sashing and border corner blocks)
1/2 yard for binding
3 1/3 yards for backing

CUTTING INSTRUCTIONS

From each solid fabric, cut (5) 3 1/8" strips; subcut (16) 3 1/8" x 7 1/8" rectangles and (16) 1 7/8" x 3 1/8" rectangles. Cut (1) 3 1/2" strip; subcut (7) 3 1/3" squares. Note: Cut the blue solid strips from the length of the fabric, not selvage to selvage.

From all the prints except the floral print for sashing: Cut (1) 3 1/8" strip; subcut (8) 3 1/8" squares. You will also need to cut (12) 1 7/8" squares.

White with red and blue print #1: Cut (2) 3 1/8" strips; subcut (16) 3 1/8" squares.

White with floral print: Cut (3) 3 1/2" strips; Subcut (31) 3 1/2" x 12 1/2" rectangles.

From the remainder cut (4) 5" squares.

CONSTRUCTING THE BLOCKS

Refer to page 110 for the steps in constructing the Comfort Quilt blocks. Begin by choosing (4) 3 1/8" squares from 2 different prints, matching a color to a solid. You will need (4) 3 1/8" x 7 1/8" rectangles and (4) 1

7/8" x 3 1/8" rectangles from the matching solid. Finally, you will need a 1 7/8" square.

You will be making 12 Comfort Quilt blocks: 4 red, 4 blue and 4 green.

PUTTING IT ALL TOGETHER

Refer to the photograph of Kimberly's quilt. Notice the placement of the solid 3 1/8" squares. Sew 5 rows of 4 solid squares separated by the 3 1/8" x 12 1/2" sashing pieces.

Notice Kimberly's arrangement of the Comfort Quilt blocks: She has created diagonal color rows. Sew 4 rows of 3 blocks, separated by the sashing pieces. Each row of blocks will begin and end with a sashing piece.

Sew the rows together, alternating a sashing row with a block row, beginning and ending with the sashing rows. Press all seam allowances toward the sashing pieces.

BORDER

Measure through the vertical and horizontal centers of the quilt top. From the length of the blue solid fabric, cut (2) 5" border strips the same length as the vertical measurement. Press the seams toward the border strip.

Cut (2) 5" border strips the same length as the horizontal measurement of your quilt top. Sew the 5" print squares to either end of both strips. Press the seam allowances toward the border strips. Sew the strips to the top and bottom, pressing the seams toward the border strips.

QUILTING

Kimberly machine quilted a meandering design over the entire surface of her quilt.

BINDING

Refer to page 122 for instructions in finishing with a straight binding.

Documenting with a label should be the last step in making your quilt.

Dogwood Trail

36" x 36"
By Dorothy Ziegler of Batesville, Ind.

*Dorothy put four Dogwood Blossom blocks on point and
added a fifth block for the center, a variation of a Courthouse Steps block.*

Refer to the Dogwood Blossom block pattern on page 16. You will need to make templates for B and C. You will need 32 copies of the foundation for paper piecing. Piece A will be rotary cut and strip pieced, following the instructions on page 113.

FABRIC REQUIREMENTS

1 1/2 yards blue solid (4-Patch units, spike background in arcs, border, center block, binding)
1/3 yard cream and blue print (4-Patch units, center block)
1 5/8 yards cream solid (setting triangles, center block, arc units)
1/8 yard blue print #1 (spikes in arcs, border)
1/8 yard blue print #2 (spikes in arcs, border)
1/8 yard blue print #3 (spikes in arcs, border)
1/8 yard blue print #4 (spikes in arcs, border)
1 1/8 yards backing

BLOCK CONSTRUCTION

4-Patch Units

This quilt has (33) 4-Patch units. Begin by making strip sets.

Blue solid: Cut (4) 2" strips
Cream and blue print: Cut (4) 2" strips

Sew each blue strip to a cream and blue strip along the long edge and press the seam allowance toward the blue print. You should have 4 strip sets 3 1/2" wide.

Crosscut the strips into segments that are 2" x 3 1/2". You need 66 segments.

Construct the 4-Patch units by pairing 2 segments, alternating dark with light. You will make (33) 4-Patch units.

Arcs

You will be making 32 arcs. Each has a solid blue background. There will be 8 arcs with spikes made from each of the blue print fabrics (one print for each arc). Half the arcs (16) will have a cream and blue print template B piece, and 16 will have blue solid template B pieces. Refer to page 119 for Paper Foundation Piecing instructions.

Blue fabric: Cut (7) 2 1/2" strips; subcut to (128) 2" x 2 1/2" rectangles for the background to the spikes. Cut (2) 2 1/2" strips; subcut to (48) 2 1/2" squares for the border. Cut 16 B template pieces.
Cream and blue fabric: Cut 16 B template pieces.
Blue print #1: Cut (1) 2 1/2" strip; subcut to (40) 1" x 2 1/2" rectangles for spikes for 1 block.
Blue print #2: Cut (1) 2 1/2" strip; subcut to (40) 1" x 2 1/2" rectangles for spikes for 1 block.
Blue print #3: Cut (1) 2 1/2" strip; subcut to (40) 1" x 2 1/2" rectangles for spikes for 1 block.
Blue print #4: Cut (1) 2 1/2" strip; subcut to (40) 1" x 2 1/2" rectangles for spikes for 1 block.
Cream solid: Cut 32 template C pieces.

Once you have each arc paper foundation pieced, you will add the B and C template pieces. Sew a blue B template piece to 4 arcs from each of the blue prints. Sew a cream and blue B template piece to the remaining 4 arcs made from the blue prints. Sew the solid cream template C pieces to each of the 32 arcs. You will have 32 arc units.

Each of the 4 Dogwood Blossom blocks in this quilt is made by combining (8) 4-Patch units and 8 arc units. All 8 arc units in the block have spikes made from the same blue print fabric. I find it best to sew the blocks together in quarters and then sew the quarters together. Remember to press the seam allowances in opposite directions. This will permit your block to lie flatter. By the way, you should have one 4-Patch unit left over. This will be used in the center block.

Center block

The center of the quilt is a variation of the Courthouse Steps block.

Cream solid: Cut (3) 2" strips; subcut to (4) 2" x 9" rectangles, (4) 2" x 7 1/2" rectangles, (4) 2" x 3 1/2" rectangles.
Blue solid: Cut (1) 2" strip; subcut to (6) 2" squares.
Cream and blue print: Cut (1) 2" strip; subcut to (6) 2" squares.

Sew a blue solid square and a cream and blue print square to the ends of 2 of the cream solid rectangles from each length.

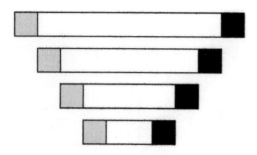

Make 2 of each

Sew a 2" x 3 1/2" rectangle to the right and left sides of the remaining 4-Patch unit.

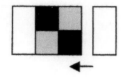

Sew the shortest rectangle unit to the top and bottom of the 4-Patch unit.

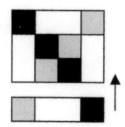

Sew the 4 3/4" rectangles to the sides of the new unit, then add the pieced rectangles to the top and bottom.

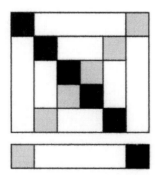

Finally, add the 2" x 9" rectangles to the sides of the unit, then add the pieced rectangles to the top and bottom. Your block should measure 12 1/2" square.

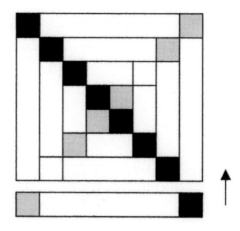

The blocks are set on point. You will need setting triangles to end up with straight sides. The corners are created by cutting 2 squares in half diagonally once. The side triangles are created by cutting 1 square in half diagonally twice. But how do you know what size squares to begin with?

You can begin by measuring your block diagonally from corner to corner. The other way is to simply multiply the length of one side of the square by 1.414 and add another 1 1/4". Sounds complicated, doesn't it?

But it isn't. You simply remember Valentine's Day, Feb. 14, which is the same as 2/14 or two 14s. Two 14s is 1414. Just add the decimal after the first 1.

So your 12" block multiplied by 1.414 is 16.968. Round that up to 17" and add another 1 1/4". That adds up to a square of 18 1/4" that you cut on the diagonal twice for the triangles on the sides. (I wish I knew who first came up with the Valentine's Day angle. Brilliant!)

The corner blocks begin with the same Valentine's Day multiplication, but then you divide that in half. Add 3/4" and you have the size of the square you cut on the diagonal once. Just remember, you'll need 2 squares for the 4 corners.

Look at the photograph of Dorothy's quilt and arrange your blocks accordingly. Sew the blocks and setting triangles into rows.

BORDER

Dorothy sewed a string of 2" squares together to create the border but discovered that the border strips were slightly too long for her top. She cleverly camouflaged the fact by reducing the size of a solid blue square in the middle of each side. The eye is drawn out to the corners and skips right over the adjustment. I suggest you do the same if you need to make adjustments.

Blue solid: Cut (48) 2" squares
Blue print #1: Cut (12) 2" squares
Blue print #2: Cut (12) 2" squares
Blue print #3: Cut (12) 2" squares
Blue print #4: Cut (12) 2" squares

Arrange the blue print squares in four stacks in front of your sewing station, along with the stack of solid blue squares. You will be sewing all but 4 of the fourth stack of blue print squares each to a solid blue square. That means you'll have solid blue squares left over, too.

Place a solid blue square on top of a print square, right sides together, and sew a 1/4" seam. Without cutting the thread, sew another pair, repeating until all but 4 squares from the fourth stack have been paired with a solid blue square. Snip the connecting thread between

each pair and stack them again in 4 stacks, keeping the blue prints together and in the same order as in the beginning. Carefully press the seam allowances toward the solid blue square. You will want to make every effort not to distort the units by pressing too aggressively.

Now sew the single squares to the solid blue square at the end of each of the units in stack #4. Be sure to keep all the strips in the same order. You don't want to alter your sequence.

Sew stack #2 to stack #1, one right after the other. Sew stack #4 to stack #3 in the same way. Clip the threads, separating the units, and press the seam allowances in the same direction as the previous pressing. Now you have 2 stacks. Sew the new stack #2 to the new stack #1, one right after the other. Separate the units and press the seam allowances in the same direction as the previous seam allowances. You should have 4 identical strings of squares and 4 solid blue squares.

Measure the vertical center of your quilt top, then measure your string of squares. If you need to adjust the border strip to fit, take a cue from Dorothy and make the adjustment in the center of the strip. Sew the adjusted strips to the sides of your quilt top. Press the seam allowances toward the border strip.

Sew a solid blue square to each end of the remaining 2 strings of squares. Press the seam allowances toward the strip, not toward the square you just added.

Measure the horizontal center of your quilt top and make any adjustments to the remaining 2 strings of squares. Because you pressed the seam allowances of the last squares you added toward the strip, the seams will nestle together snugly at the corners.

QUILTING

Dorothy hand quilted feather designs that fill triangular spaces in the solid cream areas. She quilted straight lines through rows of squares on point.

BINDING

Refer to instructions on page 122 for straight-edge binding.
Don't forget to label and document your quilt.

Constructing
the
Blocks

Constructing
THE COMFORT QUILT BLOCK

This block is constructed like a framed 9-Patch. Begin by choosing 4 squares from 1 or 2 different prints (depending on the pattern you're making), matching a color to a solid. You will need 4 larger rectangles and 4 smaller rectangles from the matching solid. Finally, you will need a small square.

The measurements for each of these pieces will be noted in the patterns. Since the patterns call for different-sized Comfort Quilt blocks, details will be listed in the pattern.

Sew 1 set of larger squares to 2 of the smaller rectangles, following the graphic below. This will be rows #1 and #3 of the 9-Patch block. Row #2 is made with the 1 smaller square and 2 smaller rectangles.

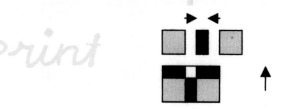

Sew a larger rectangle to either side of the 9-Patch unit. Press the seam allowance toward the rectangle.

Sew the second set of 4 larger squares to 2 of the larger rectangles, following the graphic below. Press the seam allowances toward the larger rectangles.

Sew a rectangle/square unit to the top and bottom of the 9-Patch unit, pressing the seam allowance away from the 9-Patch unit.

Constructing

THE LITTLE CEDAR TREE BLOCK

This block is so simple! It is merely a 4-Patch made from (4) 1/2-square triangle units using two fabrics.

Determine the size block you want -- let's say a 6-inch finished block. This means each of the (4) 1/2-square triangle units is 3 1/2" square.

The formula for a 1/2-square unit is finished size + seam allowance (1/2") + 3/8" (diagonal seam allowance). So a 6-inch Little Cedar block begins with (2) 3 7/8" squares, one each from two contrasting fabrics. (When I make this block, by the way, I begin with 4" squares. When the 1/2-square triangle unit is sewn, I trim to square up the unit and make it a perfect 3 1/2" square.)

Pair a dark square with a light square, right sides together. Draw a line diagonally across the wrong side of the lighter square. Sew 1/4" from the line, on both sides of the line. Cut through both layers on the line and press the seam open, pressing the seam allowance toward the darker fabric.

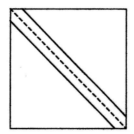

Arrange the (4) 1/2-square triangle units as in the diagram below. Sew the pairs together and press the seam allowances toward the same fabric in both sets. When you sew the two sets together, the seam allowances will oppose and the two sides will fit snugly together.

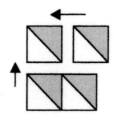

Constructing
THE MAPLE LEAF BLOCK

The Maple Leaf block consists of 4 leaf units separated by a cross that divides the block into fourths. Begin by choosing a print for the leaves and a contrasting fabric for the background. Besides squares and rectangles, the block also includes half-square triangle units.

You will need 4 large rectangles and 8 squares cut from the background fabric. You will need 13 squares from the leaf fabric. You will make 16 half-square triangle units and 4 leaf stems. The cutting instructions for each of these pieces will be listed in the individual patterns.

To make (2) 1/2-square triangle units, pair a leaf fabric square with a background fabric square, right sides together. Draw a line diagonally from corner to corner. Sew 1/4" from the line, on both sides of the line. Cut the sewn block on the line that you drew, press the units open, pressing the seam allowances toward the darker fabric. Square the unit with your rotary cutter to the size described in the pattern. You will make 16 half-square triangle units from 8 pairs of fabric squares.

An easy way to make the stem is to place a 3" length of bias tape, made with the 1/4-inch or 3/8-inch Bias Tape Maker, diagonally across the center of a background square and machine stitch or hand stitch in place. Refer to the instructions that come with your Bias Tape Maker tool for making the bias tape. You may wish to make the bias tape using the Bias Pressing Bars. Either method will work fine.

Make 4 leaf units. These are small 9-Patch blocks. The diagram below will show you the layout for the leaf block.

Sew a leaf unit to either side of 2 large rectangles. Sew a large rectangle to either side of the small square. Sew the 3 rows together, referring to the Maple Leaf pattern on page 13. Notice that the stems of the leaves all radiate from the center square.

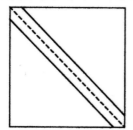

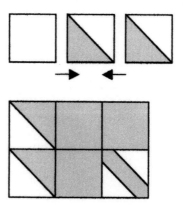

Constructing
THE SPIDER WEB BLOCK

STRIP PIECING

You certainly may construct this block using the templates provided in "Pick a Pack – Pick a Pattern." However, I always like to "strip piece" whenever possible and cut with the rotary cutter and ruler. In the long run, my piecing is more accurate.

I know this method will result in lots of extra fabric when I'm finished. You might use the leftovers for a second quilt design. In the second quilt design, the "circle" in the center of the block will appear smaller than in the original design.

You will find a variety of specialty rulers at your local quilt shop that are cut in the shape of the triangle in the Spider Web block. The staff at the shop can tell you how they work. I'm partial to one that is marked with lines that tell me how wide I need to cut or piece strips before cutting the triangles. The ruler also has markings for cutting the right-sized strips for the 1/2-square triangles to complete the block.

For a 12" Spider Web block, you will need a 2 1/2" strip and 4 7/8" strip from each of your light and dark fabrics. Sew a light strip to a dark strip and press the seam allowance toward the darker fabric. This will place the seam allowances in opposite directions as you sew the wedges together, which is desirable when sewing 4-Patch blocks.

Using your specialty ruler (sometimes referred to as a Kaleidoscope ruler), cut the wedges, 4 from each strip set per block. Sew 4 wedges together to form half the Spider Web, taking care to sew with an accurate 1/4" seam allowance. Press all seam allowances in the same direction.

Sew the remaining 4 wedges together, then sew the halves together. I recommend beginning at the center and sewing out to the edge, then starting in the center and sewing out to the other edge. You will have an easier time matching all the points in the center. Pressing all the seam allowances in the same direction around the center will let the middle of the block lay flatter, because the bulk is distributed evenly.

Finally, add the 1/2-square triangles to create the corners.

TEMPLATE PIECING

Using the templates, you may construct these blocks with your sewing machine or you may piece them by hand.

For each block you will need 4 dark template A shapes, 4 light and 4 dark template B shapes and 4 light and 4 dark template C shapes. Begin by sewing the light template B shapes to the dark template C shapes and the dark template B shapes to the light template C shapes for 8 wedges.

Press the seam allowances toward the dark fabric each time so the seams will butt up against each other tightly when you sew the wedges together.

Alternate the lights and darks and sew the wedges together in pairs. Sew 2 pairs together to form a half, then sew the halves together. Begin in the center, where all the points come together, and sew toward the outer edge in one direction, then repeat in the other direction. Your center will be more accurate. As with the strip-pieced block, press all the seam allowances in the same direction around the center.

Add the template A shapes to the corners, taking care to add the dark corners to the wedges with the light template B shapes.

Constructing

THE DOGWOOD BLOSSOM BLOCK

FOUNDATION PAPER PIECED ARC UNITS

Tools needed for Paper Foundation Piecing

As many paper copies of the foundation as necessary needed for the blocks you are making.

Sewing machine with #14 needle

"Add-a-Quarter" Ruler (6" length is fine)

Pressing stick (I actually use a Hera Marker)

Flat flower head pins (you need only 2 or 3)

Rotary cutter with new or newly sharpened blade (28 mm)

Rotary cutting mat no smaller than this book page

Small scissors

Begin by reproducing the arc foundation pattern as many times as the pattern directs. Be sure to add enough foundation around each pattern to accommodate a 1/4"-inch seam allowance. Each Dogwood Blossom takes (8) arc units unless otherwise noted.

Each arc takes (4) 2" x 2 1/2" rectangles for the background and (5) 1" x 2" rectangles for the spikes. Determine how many arcs from any two fabrics you need and cut strips accordingly. You will get (40) spike pieces from each 2-inch strip, cut selvage to selvage, and you will get (20) background pieces from each 2 1/2-inch strip, cut selvage to selvage. The fabric requirement for each pattern has been figured accordingly, and an extra strip has been added in case of cutting mistakes.

You will be working on both sides of the foundation. You will do all your machine sewing on the side with the lines defining the arc. The "wrong" side of the foundation is actually the one on which your fabric pieces will be sewn.

Please note: In foundation piecing, the finished block is in mirror image. For instance, if you want to place your colors, shading from light to dark and, from the left of the arc to the right, you must sew the fabric in what appears to be the complete opposite order.

The arc pattern on page 132 shows the letter D, E or F within each shape. These letters represent templates, in case you wish to create templates to hand piece the arc unit. For foundation piecing, you will want to number the patches starting on one end and numbering straight around the arc. In other words, the F on one end is #1, the D right next to it is #2, the E that follows is #3 and so on. The F on the other end is #9.

Place a 1" x 2" rectangle of the spike fabric on the wrong side of the pattern, wrong side of fabric against the foundation, covering the patch represented by #1. Make sure that all sides of the patch are covered. You will have to position from the front of the pattern to see that you are covering the patch. I try to "eyeball" a 1/4-" inch seam allowance that overlaps into patch #2. Pin in place with a flat flower-head pin, pinning far enough away from the sewing line so you do not as not to hit it with the machine foot.

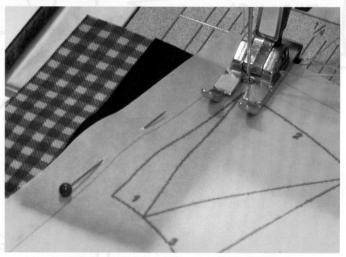

Place a 2" x 2 1/2" rectangle of spike background fabric on the wrong side of the pattern, aligning the long edge with the fabric that is already pinned in place, right sides together, centering the fabric on the patch #2, not on the fabric of #1. When you sew on the line and fold the fabric piece back, it must totally cover the patch #2, with excess all around for seam allowance. You may pin this piece as you did #1, or simply hold it carefully and turn the whole thing over.

Sew on the line that separates patch #1 and patch #2. Begin stitching just behind the line a couple of stitches and end in front of the line a couple of stitches. I always align the line with my needle, drop the needle and then drop the foot. Trying to move the foundation after the foot is down just doesn't work.

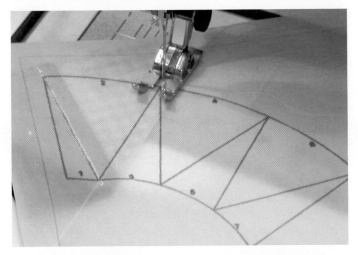

Turn the foundation over and fold the patch #2 fabric open, pulling it tight against the stitching, and press with the pressing stick or Hera Marker. Turn the foundation over and determine the next line on which you will sew. This will be the line that separates #2 and #3. Fold the foundation back on this line, exposing the fabric from patch #2. With the Add-a-Quarter ruler oriented over the fold so the little ledge that determines the 1/4"-inch is right against the folded foundation, use your a rotary cutter to trim the excess fabric. This will give you a perfect 1/4" seam allowance when sewing patch #3.

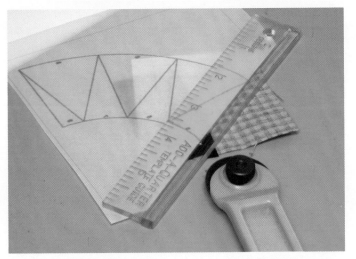

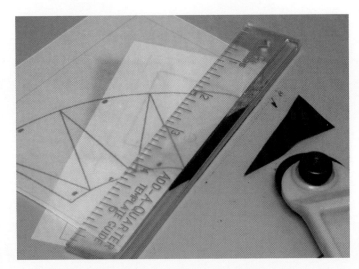

Turn the foundation over again and align a 1" x 2" rectangle of spike fabric with the newly cut edge of the previous patch, right sides together, centering the rectangle against the patch on the foundation labeled #3.

Repeat the previous steps until you complete #9. After pressing #9 open, turn the foundation over and sew about 5 stitches in the seam allowance to hold the patch #9 securely against the foundation. If you don't tack it in place, the fabric may shift when you trim the arc. Trim the arc unit, adding a 1/4" seam allowance if your foundation doesn't already include it.

4-Patch Units

An easy way to make multiple 4-Patch units of the same fabrics is to sew strips sets and then cut the strip sets into segments. Each of the patterns that calls for the 4-Patch units will tell you how many strips to cut and which strips to sew together. The pattern will also tell you in which direction to press the seam allowance.

Sew the (2) 2" strips together along the long edge. Press the seam allowance toward one of the strips, being very careful not to you don't distort the strip set, causing the set to "frown." The strip set should measure 3 1/2" wide unless otherwise noted in the pattern. Subcut the strip set into 2" segments.

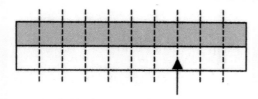

Pair two of the segments, alternating the direction of one, and sew together. The seam allowances of the segments will be opposing, allowing the segments to fit snuggly at the intersecting seam.

Release the stitches in the seam allowance and press the seam allowances in the opposite directions. Each of the seam allowances will be pressed in the same direction around the center. The backside of the 4-Patch unit will look like the graphic below.

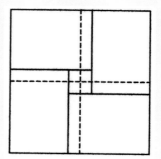

The 4-Patch units should measure 3 1/2" square unless otherwise noted in the pattern.

The Techniques

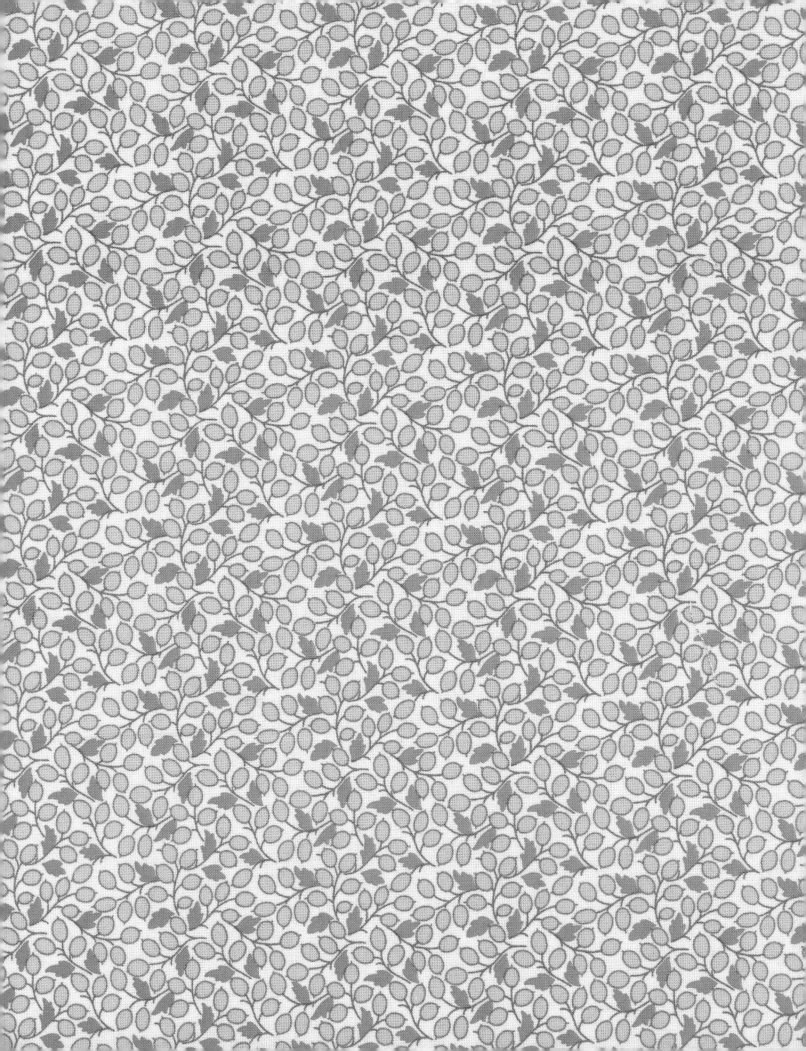

PAPER FOUNDATION PIECING

The most important thing to remember with foundation piecing is that much of what you know about block piecing must be forgotten. In foundation piecing you align pieces not to each other but to the foundation. Your fabric pieces cover "patches" on the foundation and in doing so create the design. Depending on whether your foundation is paper or fabric, you may or may not be removing it once the block is constructed.

When I teach this process I remind my students to think "teaspoon." That is, TSP: Trim, Stitch, Press. I also have them ask themselves, "What is my next sewing line?" This keeps them straight.

Set your sewing machine for 17-18 stitches per inch, 1.5 on European machines. If stitching on a paper foundation, you will want to use a larger needle – a 90/14.

Begin by determining your sewing line. The first one will be between the first patch to cover and the second. After that it will be between the area you have covered and the next patch to add. The numbering on the foundation pattern will determine the stitching sequence.

When making the arc units for the Dogwood Blossom blocks, begin with a rectangle. You'll find cutting dimensions in each pattern. Place the fabric piece on the wrong side of the foundation, wrong side of the fabric against the wrong side of the foundation pattern, covering the "patch #1" and extending just 1/4" into patch #2. (You can "eyeball" the 1/4" or you can use your ruler to trim it to a perfect 1/4" after aligning the fabric. I find that "eyeballing" it is fine.) Pin the fabric in place, keeping the pin well away from the line on which you'll sew.

Place the second piece of fabric, right side together with the first piece, aligning the edge. The piece is centered on the patch, not on the fabric, so they may appear askew.

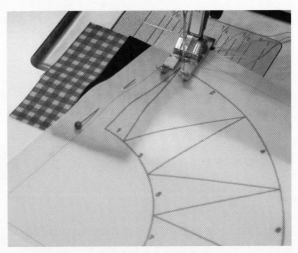

Stitch on the line from the paper side. The fabric will be underneath, against the feed dogs. Begin your line of stitching and end in the seam allowance. That is, begin a stitch or two before the line on the pattern begins and end a stitch or two after the line on the pattern ends. Subsequent seams will lock the stitching so you won't need to backstitch.

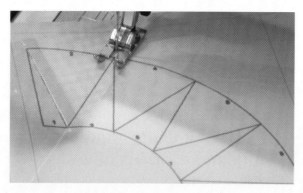

Fold back the patch of fabric and press. I use a Hera Marker instead of an iron. The heat of the iron will transfer the ink from the foundation pattern to the ironing board and eventually onto your fabric.

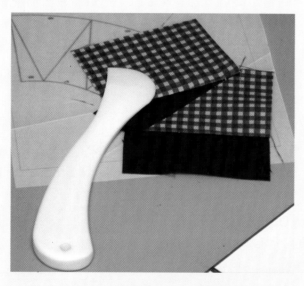

Determine your next seam line. Fold the foundation back on that line. Place a ruler's 1/4" line, or a special ruler designed for foundation piecing called the Add-a-Quarter Ruler from CM Designs, on the fold and trim away the excess with the rotary cutter. This creates a 1/4" seam allowance against which to align the next piece of fabric.

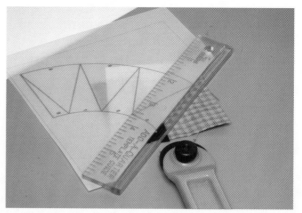

Align your next piece on the newly created 1/4" seam allowance, remembering that you are aligning the fabric with the foundation pattern, not necessarily the previous piece of fabric.

Stitch on the line, beginning and ending with a couple of stitches in the seam allowance.

Determine your next seam line and proceed as described: Trim, Stitch, Press. When the block is complete, trim the excess away, leaving a 1/4" seam allowance all around. If the pieces at the corners or on the edges are loose, they may shift when you trim. Tack the fabric to the foundation in the seam allowance before trimming. You really need to make only about 5 stitches.

MITERED CORNERS

Begin by measuring through the vertical center of your quilt top. Cut strips for the side borders the same length as the vertical center of the quilt top plus the width of 2 border strips. I always add a few inches for good measure.

Find the center of the border edge and mark with a pin. Measure from the center out toward the end. Find the center of the border strip by folding it in half lengthwise and mark with a pin.

Measure to the end of the strip and mark with a pin to represent the corners. Fold the halves in half and find the center, marking with a pin. Repeat to find the quarters of the edge of the quilt top. Matching all the pins, pin the border strip to the sides of the quilt top. Sew the strips to the quilt top with a 1/4" seam allowance, beginning and ending 1/4" from the end. Press the seam allowances toward the border strips.

Measure the horizontal middle of your quilt top with the side borders added. This is the length to cut the top and bottom borders plus a couple inches for good measure. Find the matching points as you did with the first set of strips and sew to the top and bottom, again beginning and ending 1/4" from the end. Press the seam allowances toward the border strips.

Now you're ready to work on the corners. Working on the ironing board is convenient, as you will want to use the iron. With right sides together, fold the quilt top diagonally, lining up the top edge with the right edge. Perfectly align the seams that attach the borders, placing a few pins along the seams to secure. Place a long ruler on the diagonal fold, extending it over the border strips. With a pen-cil, trace a line on the border strips that exactly extends the line of the fold. This line will be 45 degrees from the outside edge of the border. Place a few pins across the line to secure against slippage when you move the quilt to your sewing machine.

Fold back the seam allowance between the quilt top and the border to expose the beginning point of the previous seams. You will sew right on the line you drew. I find that if I sew from the seam out to the corner, the corner will stretch slightly. I suggest beginning at the outside corner and sewing toward the seam, stopping at the seam and not catching the seam allowance, then backstitching a couple of stitches to secure.

Back at the ironing board, press open the seam allowance you just stitched. Trim the excess fabric to a 1/4" allowance. Press the inside corner flat. Repeat this sequence for the remaining 3 corners.

STRAIGHT BINDING

Depending on the batting you have chosen, or the loft, cut strips for your binding either 2 1/2" or 2 1/4" wide. To determine the number of strips you will need, measure the top edge and a side, multiply by 2 (to get the circumference of your quilt top) and divide by 40 (the average usable length of a strip cut selvage to selvage, after the selvage is removed). Naturally a partial strip should be counted as a whole strip. If the number you get is 5.666, you would cut 6 strips.

To determine the amount of fabric I need to buy for the binding, I then multiply the number of strips I need by the 2 1/2" width of the binding strip and round up about 1/8 yard. This gives me enough to straighten the fabric before I begin cutting strips, or even to make a mistake! (I always multiply by 2 1/2" even if I'm going to make the strips 2 1/4" wide.) So, say I need 6 strips. That's 15 inches. I'll round up to 1/2 yard (18") and that will give me another strip should I need it. If had needed exactly 18" I would still have rounded up so that I would have extra "just in case."

Remove the selvages and sew the strips together on the bias across the tails, not through them.

Trim the excess so that you have a 1/4" seam allowance and press the seam open. This will help to eliminate bulk. Press the entire strip in half (the full length) wrong side in. Now you're ready to bind you quilt.

I do not trim away the excess or backing before adding the binding, but I do make sure that the corners are square. Using your 12 1/2" square ruler, mark the corners square if they have been distorted at all. When sewing the binding to the quilt, let this line guide you in the corners, not the edge of the quilt top.

Fit your sewing machine with the walking foot or even-feed foot. Move the needle to the far right position so that it is 1/4" to 3/8" from the edge of the foot. The edge of the foot will be your sewing guide. At this point I have not removed any excess batting or backing. I wait to do that after the binding is attached. I also increase the length of my stitches just a bit since I'm sewing through more thickness than when I piece.

Begin in the center of a side. Putting the raw edges of the binding to the edge of the quilt top or the marking you made for the square corner and leaving a 10"-12" tail, sew the binding to the corner but not all the way through the corner. Stop the same distance from the corner that your needle is from the edge of the quilt, 1/4" to 3/8".

Pull the quilt out from under the needle and turn the quilt so that you will be sewing the next edge. Fold the binding at a 45-degree angle from the stitched part. The raw edge of the binding and the raw edge of the quilt top will form a straight line. If not, it is probably because I stitched beyond where I should have. If that's the case, I clip that last stitch. This allows me to pull the binding back farther so that I do make that straight line. If you're straight, then fold the binding down over the corner, lining the raw edge with the new side. Begin sewing again from the edge to just before the next corner and repeat.

When you get to the final side, stop sewing 12" to 15" from where you began. At this point there are several ways to finish, but some of them are bulkier than others. The method I use isn't really hard once you get the hang of it and it gives a smooth join. So let me walk you through this slowly. Once you get it, you'll be delighted with the technique.

Bring the two tails together in the middle of the unsewn space. Fold the tails back on themselves so that there is a gap of about 1/8" between the two where the folds meet. Make a small clip though all 4 layers of binding fabric where they meet in the center, perpendicular to the raw edge. Be sure that your clip is no deeper than about 1/8". You don't want to clip through where you will be sewing your seam.

Now place your quilt on the table so that the edge on which you are working is right in front of you and the rest of the quilt is across the table. Open the left tail. The right side will be toward the quilt top and the wrong side will be showing. Place your left hand, palm up, on the quilt top behind the open binding

(the binding is between you and your hand). With your right hand, flip the tail over, toward your hand, so that the wrong side of the binding is now in your hand and the right side is facing up. Angle the end of the tail toward the center of your quilt.

Open the right tail so that the wrong side is facing up and angle it toward the center of the quilt top. Now place the right tail on top of the left tail. Cross them at a 45-degree angle to each other. Match the clips you made so the correct placement occurs. Place a pin to hold the matched points in place. You will be sewing across the tails, so place your pin perpendicular to the sewing line.

Press the seam open and trim to a 1/4" seam allowance. Fold the binding again as you had it in the beginning and press the seam. Align the raw edges to the quilt top and finish sewing the binding to the top between the point where you began and ended. You should notice that the binding is flat and smooth!

Once the binding is attached, you are ready to remove the excess batting and backing. I always want to be sure the batting completely fills my binding. To that end I cut the excess, leaving about 1/8" extending past the raw edge of the binding.

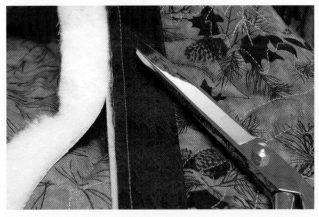

To stitch the binding, fold the finished edge around the raw edge to the back, just covering the machine stitching. You won't have to pin all the binding to the back, but you will find that securing some as you're working will keep the fabric from stretching. Some quilters use pins, pinning in the direction they stitch so they don't prick knuckles. My favorite aids are "binding clips" that, for a previous generation, acted as hair clips! You will find these marvelous tools at your local quilt shop.

At the corners, tuck the fold that is created by the mitered corner in the opposite direction of the fold on the front side. This will distribute the bulk so that the corner is smoother. If the binding gaps in the corner, stitch the fold. This will make an even neater corner.

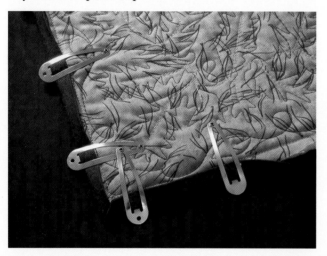

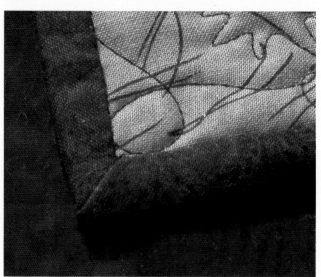

I suggest that you sew with a sharp or straw needle and match the thread to the binding fabric. Hide the knot on the underside of the binding and sew the binding to the back of the quilt, hiding the machine stitches. Take a small stitch in the back, being careful not to go all the way through to the front, and then bring the needle through the edge of the binding, right in the fold. The stitch will be hidden in the fabric. The stitches should be short and close together so that the binding is secure.

SCALLOPED BORDER AND BIAS BINDING

While the scalloped edge is not the most difficult quilting technique, it does require some patience to achieve.

The first thing to consider is how much fabric you need for the binding. Begin by choosing a scallop. You will have different-shaped scallops for the sides and the corners. They each may measure differently.

To measure a scallop, use a piece of string or a flexible measuring tape. Place the measuring device around the edge of a scallop and measure the length of the string or tape. Multiply that measurement by the number of the scallops that size and you have the partial length of the outside edge of your quilt. (You'll notice in the photograph that my scallop measures 17 1/2". It won't hurt for me to round that up to 18" per scallop.) In the same way, measure the 4 corners and add that to your first measurement and you'll have the full perimeter of the quilt.

Because of the curves of the scallops, you will want to make binding strips from bias-cut strips.

The binding I recommend is a double-folded binding for durability. Most of my binding strips begin as 2" or 2 1/4" strips. On occasion I use 2 1/2" strips, but only if the batting has a higher loft or the fabric is a little thicker, such as flannel.

To determine the amount of bias binding fabric you need, multiply the perimeter of your quilt by the width of the bias strip you'll use. On a calculator, find the button with a symbol similar to this: √ Your calculator may have the letters "sqrt" on a button. Either one is the button that will find the square root of the number that appears in the display window. Hit that button after you multiply the perimeter by the strip width. Now, round that number up to the next even number and you will have the size of the square of fabric that you'll need to make the binding.

Let's say your side scallops measure 18" and

there are 4 on each side of the quilt and each corner scallop measures 20". That means your perimeter is 368 inches. Let's say you want your bias strips to measure 2 1/4" wide. When you multiply the two numbers you get 828. The square root of 828 is 28.774. So we round that up to the next highest even number and we get 30 inches. We want a 30" square, which means you need to purchase 7/8 yard of binding fabric.

When you slice that 30" piece of fabric into bias strips, you will notice that several strips from opposite corners are shorter than the majority of strips. I prefer to have the strips as long as possible and not use the short strips. Short strips mean many seams. I always purchase an extra 3/4 to 1 yard of my binding fabric. I don't mind having leftovers, but I do mind those seams. Buying extra means I can get most of the strips I need out of the full width of the fabric.

Measure one of the strips and divide that into the perimeter (remember that 828 inches in the example?) to find how many strips you need. I always add an extra strip for good measure so I'll have plenty for the final join.

I must fold the fabric in half on the bias so I am able to cut across the full width of the fabric on the bias. I don't have a ruler long enough to cross the full width of fabric, which is about 62." I don't even have a ruler that will cross the half, actually. You may be tempted to make the fold twice. To do that you must be very careful that both folds are perfectly parallel or you will end up with a W of a strip instead of a straight strip. I don't trust myself to make both folds line up that way, so I just make the one fold. Instead, I use two rulers, end to end, and cut very carefully and slowly, walking my anchoring hand up the ruler as the rotary cutter becomes parallel to my fingertips.

There are directions in various places for making a "continuous bias" strip. This involves cutting a square in half on the diagonal and sewing the two pieces back together again, altering the grain of the piece. Then you draw lines every 2 1/4", sew the ends together matching the lines but skewing them, creating a spiral, and then cut the line around the spiral. Doing so results in a continuous bias strip. For such a large piece of fabric, I would rather cut the strips with a rotary cutter and rotary cutting ruler. I really don't mind sewing the strips end to end. This is a matter of preference and you should do what is best for you. Either method is correct.

Once your binding strips are sewn together, press the seam allowances open, trim to 1/4" and press the strip in half, wrong side in, the full length of the binding. Be sure as you press the crease in that you don't stretch the strips. Don't iron, press – up and down motions with the iron, not side to side.

Leaving a 12" or 15" tail, begin pinning the raw edges of the binding to the edge of the scallop on the downside of the scallop. Don't begin at the highest point of the scallop but about halfway between the highest and lowest point. (Please note: As I begin, I have not trimmed any excess away. I always trim after I have sewn on the binding, whether it is a straight binding or a scalloped edge.)

As you pin the binding to the curve of the scallop, be very careful that you do not stretch the binding by pulling it. The raw edge will stretch a little because you are making a straight edge curve. However, there is a fine line you must not cross. Think of the binding strip as three layers. The first layer, the raw edge, will stretch slightly in its space. The second layer, the body of the strip, will not stretch at all. The third layer, the folded edge, will actually scrunch a little. This is a good thing because when the folded edge gets pulled to the back, it needs to be able to stretch a little.

Pin only as far as the first pivot point, the deepest part of the V between scallops, and begin sewing. I recommend a 1/4" or 3/8" seam allowance, depending on how wide you made your bias strips. I always use the even-feed foot on my sewing machine for sewing on binding and I sew very slowly. I do sew over the pins, although I know you are not supposed to. Machine makers just cringe at the thought! I once heard that a new, sharp needle is more likely to slide over the side of a pin than hit it and break, so I make sure I start with a new needle and I sew slowly. I've never broken a needle in this process. If you sew slowly enough, you can pull the pins just as you get to them and not sew over them. I recommend you leave the pin in until the needle is just about to sew over it, though. You don't want the fabric to shift, causing a pleat in the binding.

If your machine has a "needle down" setting, set it for down. This way as you stop sewing the needle stays in the lowest position. When you lift the foot to reposition your quilt, you won't have to worry that you've moved away from the line of sewing. If you don't have this setting on your machine, advance the wheel by hand until the needle is in its lowest position before you reposition. Be careful you don't tug on the quilt, pulling the needle to bend it. You'll break it for sure.

Sew until you get to the deepest point of the V and stop with the needle in its lowest position.

If the pins are still in the binding you've sewn, take them out. Now start pinning the next scallop. The folded edge of the binding will want to stand up a bit at the V, but don't worry about it. Just remember you don't want to pull the binding to stretch it. Carefully pin the binding to the next scallop until you reach the next V.

To begin sewing, turn the quilt and make one stitch parallel to the straight of the grain of the border and then pivot again to stitch the curve of the scallop. This one little stitch will relieve some of the stress that will be put on the pivot point. Before you begin stitching the next scallop, you will want to move the seam allowance of the sewn binding out of the way. To do this, use a stiletto, or even the tip of a seam ripper, to grip the seam allowance and fold it back on itself. Since it is basically under your feed foot, you won't be able to reach it with your finger. Continue sewing the binding to your scallops all the way around the quilt, ending about halfway between the last V and the highest point of the scallop. You will again want a 12" to 15" tail. (Refer to page 123 to make a smooth join of the tails.)

Fold the folded edge of the binding to the back of your quilt and hand stitch with an invisible stitch to secure, hiding the machine stitching. Match your thread to the binding to camouflage the stitching.

When you get to the V at the deepest part of the scallops, you will want to miter the binding. Clip into the V through all the layers of the seam allowance. You do not need to clip all the way to the stitching, just about halfway. This clip gives you some working room with the fold that will be created in the binding.

As you get to the deepest part of the V, take a tuck in the binding so you have a nice crisp point in the V. I make the tuck on the back in the opposite direction of the tuck on the front. Stitch the fold the tuck creates just as you do on the corners of the straight, mitered binding corners, front and back. Your binding will be very neat, and the edge of your quilt will look very crisp.

Paper
Foundations

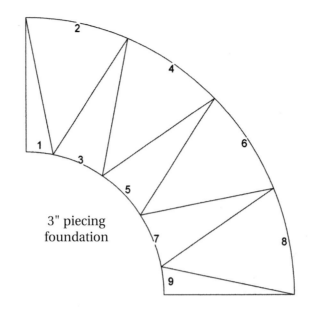

3" piecing
foundation

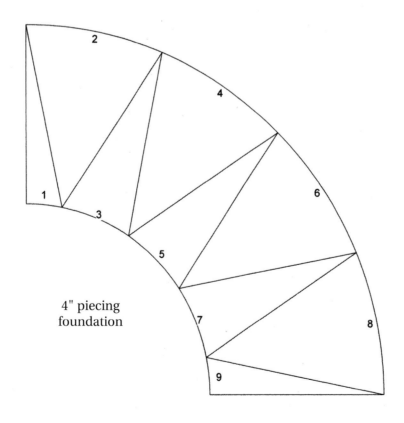

4" piecing
foundation

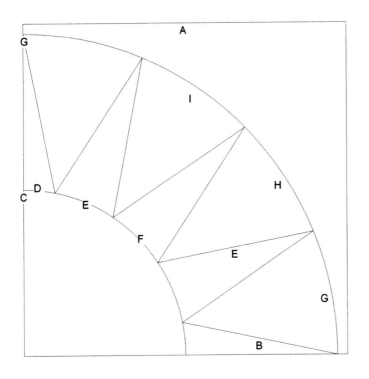

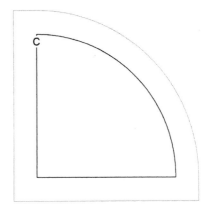

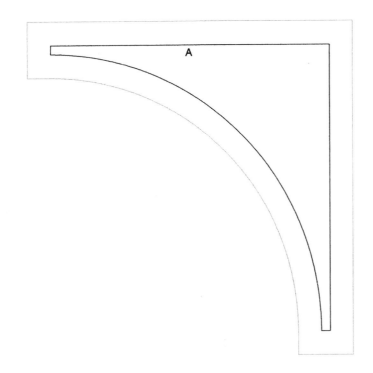

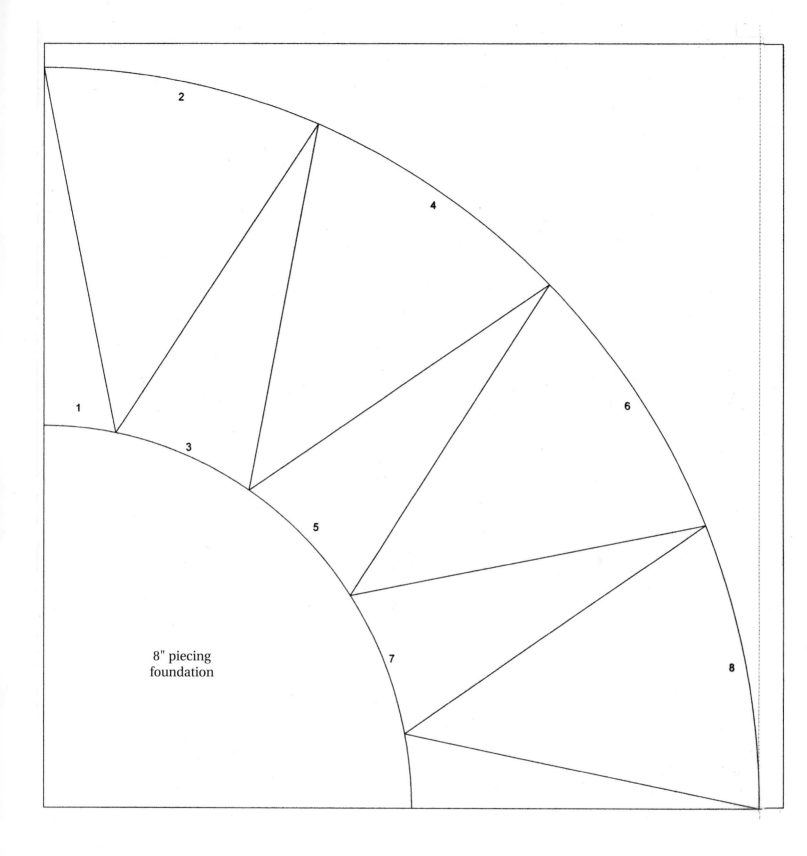

8" piecing
foundation

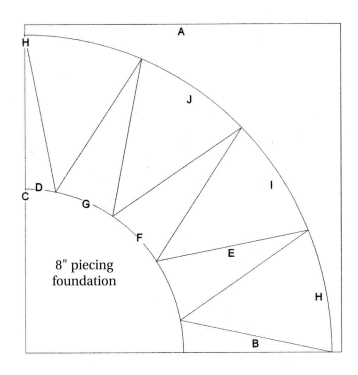

8" piecing
foundation

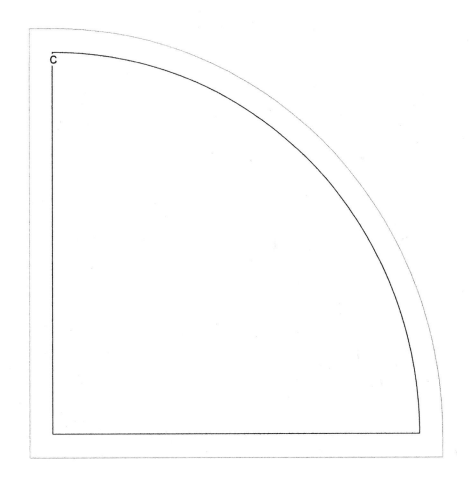

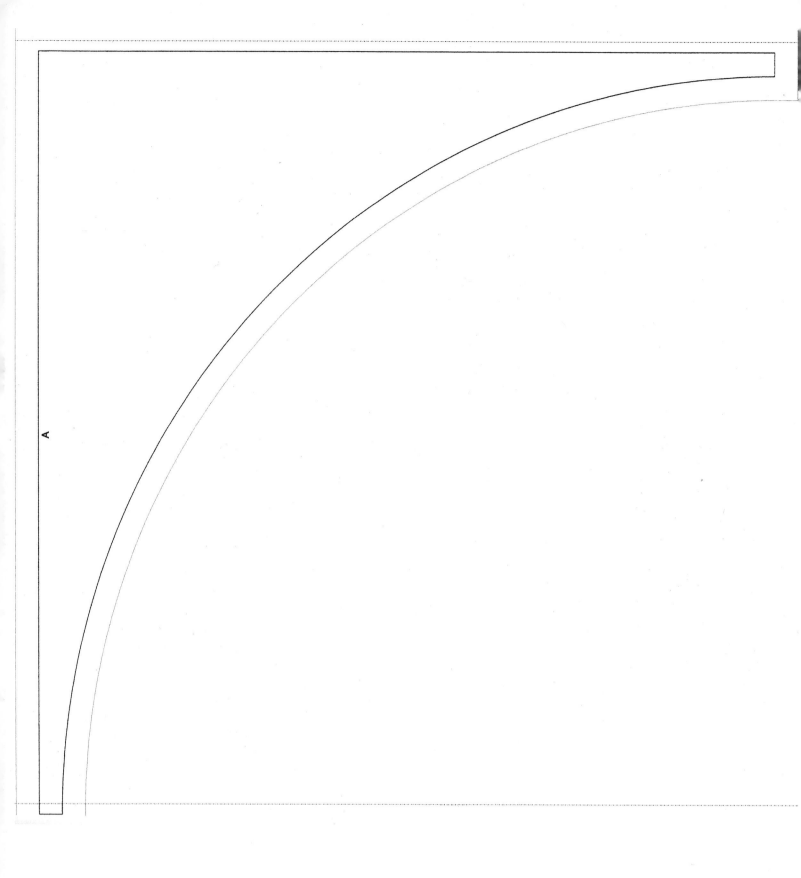

A

Kansas City Star Quilts
THE BOOKS

Star Quilts I: *One Piece at a Time* by Kansas City Star Books – 1999.

Star Quilts II: *More Kansas City Star Quilts* by Edie McGinnis - 2000

Star Quilts III: *Outside the Box: Hexagon Patterns from The Kansas City Star* by Edie McGinnis – 2001.

Star Quilts IV: *Prairie Flower: A Year on the Plains* by Barbara Brackman – 2001.

Star Quilts V: *The Sister Blocks* by Edie McGinnis – 2001.

Star Quilts VI: *Kansas City Quiltmakers* by Doug Worgul – 2001.

Star Quilts VII: *O'Glory: Americana Quilt Blocks from The Kansas City Star* by Edie McGinnis – 2001.

Star Quilts VIII: *Hearts & Flowers: Hand Applique From Start to Finish* by Kathy Delany – 2002.

Star Quilts IX: *Roads & Curves Ahead* by Edie McGinnis – 2002.

Star Quilts X: *Celebration of American Life: Applique Patterns Honoring a Nation and Its People* by Barb Adams and Alma Allen – 2002.

Star Quilts XI: *Women of Grace & Charm: A Quilting Tribute to the Women Who Served in World War II* by Barb Adams and Alma Allen – 2003.

Star Quilts XII: *A Heartland Album: More Techniques in Hand Applique* by Kathy Delany – 2003.

Star Quilts XIII: *Quilting a Poem: Designs Inspired by America's Poets* by Frances Kit and Debra Rowden – 2003.

Star Quilts XIV: *Carolyn's Paper-Pieced Garden: Patterns for Miniature and Full-Sized Quilts* by Carolyn Cullinan McCormack – 2003.

Star Quilts XV: *Murders On Elderberry Road,* a mystery book by Sally Goldenbaum – 2003.

Star Quilts XVI: *Friendships in Bloom: Round Robin Quilts* by Marjorie Nelson & Rebecca Nelson-Zerfas - 2003.

Star Quilts XVII: *Baskets of Treasures: Designs Inspired by Life Along the River* by Edie McGinnis – 2003.

Star Quilts XVIII: *Heart & Home: Unique American Women and the Houses that Inspire* by Kathy Schmitz – 2003.

Star Quilts XIX: *Women of Design: Quilts in the Newspaper* by Barbara Brackman – 2004.

Star Quilts XX: *The Basics: An Easy Guide to Beginning Quiltmaking* by Kathy Delaney – 2004.

Star Quilts XXI: *Four Block Quilts: Echoes of History, Pieced Boldly & Appliquéd Freely* by Terry Clothier Thompson – 2004.

Kansas City Star Quilts

THE BOOKS

Star Quilts XXII: *No Boundaries: Bringing Your Fabric Over The Edge*
   by Edie McGinnis – 2004.

Star Quilts XXIII: *Horn of Plenty for a New Century* by Kathy Delaney – 2004.

Star Quilts XXIV: *Quilting the Garden* by Barb Adams and Alma Allen – 2004.

Star Quilts XXV: *A Murder of Taste: A Queen Bee Quilt Mystery*
   by Sally Goldenbaum - 2004

Star Quilts XXVI: *Patterns of History: Moda Fabric Challenge* by Barbara
   Brackman – 2004.

Star Quilts XXVII: *Stars All Around Us: Quilts and Projects Inspired by a Beloved
   Symbol* by Cherie Ralston – 2005.

Star Quilts XXVIII: *Quilters' Stories: Collecting History in the Heart of America*
   by Debra Rowden – 2005.

Star Quilts XXIX: *Libertyville* by Terry Clothier Thompson – 2005.

Star Quilts XXX: *Sparkling Jewels, Pearls of Wisdom* by Edie McGinnis – 2005.

Star Quilts XXXI: *Grapefruit Juice and Sugar* by Jenifer Dick – 2005.

Star Quilts XXXII: *Home Sweet Home* by Barb Adams and Alma Allen – 2005.

Star Quilts XXXIII: *Patterns of History, The Challenge Winners*
   by Kathy Delaney – 2005

Project books:

Santa's Parade of Nursery Rhymes by Jeanne Poore – 2000.

Fan Quilt Memories: A Selection of Fan Quilts from The Kansas City Star
   by Jeanne Poore – 2001.